T0326523

Germany's Creative Sector and its Impact on Employment Growth

Structural Change and Structural Policies

Edited by Prof. Wolfram Elsner and Dr. Henning Schwardt

Volume 22

PETER LANG

Frankfurt am Main · Berlin · Bern · Bruxelles · New York · Oxford · Wien

Jan Wedemeier

Germany's Creative Sector and its Impact on Employment Growth

A Theoretical and Empirical Approach
to the Fuzzy Concept of Creativity:
Richard Florida's Arguments Reconsidered

PETER LANG
Internationaler Verlag der Wissenschaften

Bibliographic Information published by the Deutsche Nationalbibliothek
The Deutsche Nationalbibliothek lists this publication in the Deutsche Nationalbibliografie; detailed bibliographic data is available in the internet at http://dnb.d-nb.de.

Zugl.: University of Bremen, Diss., Dr. rer. pol., 2012

First supervisor: Prof. Dr. Wolfram Elsner,
University of Bremen and Institute of Institutional and Innovation Economics (iino), Germany
Second supervisor: Prof. Dr. Michael Bräuninger,
Helmut-Schmidt University Hamburg and Hamburg Institute of International Economics (HWWI), Germany
Date of colloquium 2012.01.24

Cover design:
© Olaf Glöckler, Atelier Platen, Friedberg

D 46
ISSN 1438-2644
ISBN 978-3-631-63582-7

© Peter Lang GmbH
Internationaler Verlag der Wissenschaften
Frankfurt am Main 2012
All rights reserved.

www.peterlang.de

The Book Series "Structural Change and Structural Policies"

"Structural change", and particularly "global" structural change, is a ubiquitous and topical issue. Indeed, it is the phenomenon that reflects the *dynamics* and *complex evolution* of the economy most immediately and comprehensively—and, in turn, is at the basis of economic growth and evolution. Also, economic policy has become much more "structural policy", or better: a whole spread of "structural policies", in recent decades, rather than just aggregate or macro management.

Viewed *statically* and *statistically*, "structure" and "structural change" mirror socioeconomic phenomena simply at a *"middle" range of aggregation: Industries*, sectors, branches, industrial-spatial *clusters* and firm *networks*, furthermore *regions*, and, finally, statistical *size ranges of firms* (the class of mini and "micro" units, including spin-offs or new firm start-ups, further the renowned "small and medium-sized firms" group or layer, up to the large companies and the "transnational corporations", another research area of its own). Corresponding structural policies would comprise *industrial policies*, including nowadays a broad support for *start-ups* and "entrepreneurship", *cluster- and network-*oriented development strategies as well as related *innovation* policy and some *"human capital"* development policy. They also contain *regional policies*, again today mostly cluster- and network-based, sometimes aiming at *spatially even* living conditions and regional *convergence*, sometimes aiming at strengthening the strong *metropolitan growth centres* (mostly pursuing both of these contradictory objectives at a time, though).

Viewed *dynamically*, or better: in an *evolutionary complexity perspective* of an economic systems under scrutiny, structural change and structural policies relate to complex systems based on *direct*, and often highly *problematic interdependencies*, i.e., relations among agents that are not only indirect and existing just through ideal "market equilibrium" prices (given through the summed-up simultaneous decisions of *all* agents, demanders and suppliers). Direct and collective, thus often *dilemma-prone interdependencies* immediately imply complex and *truly uncertain decision situations*. They trigger, and their solutions in fact require, processes that in turn can not be characterised just in terms of prices and quantities exchanged. Most basically, different and diverse, and often most complicated, *coordination problems* are involved that often do require *cooperative action* by the agents. Cooperative action, in turn, can emerge only in a process of *recurrent interaction*, with *interactive learning* and emerging related *expectations* ("trust"). It will not evolve on the basis of ideal short-run (hyper-) rationality but through the learning from experience of some other, a *long-run* rationality, given enough bearing, and awareness, of a *common futurity*. This new rationality, however, can evolve only as a long-run semiconscious *habituation*, a social rule or informal *social institution*. This is the perspective of *evolutionary-institutional* complexity economics.

Informal institutions make *cooperation* in ubiquitous complex *social dilemma* situations feasible. Typically, such "trust" and cooperation emerges in a spontaneous historical process in industrial-spatial *clusters* that typically exclude turbulent price-related "market" exchanges in their idiosyncratic interrelations. Based on such "raw material", i.e., trust emerging in clusters, *networks*, then, are multilateral, project-based and deliberately agreed forms of ("strategic") cooperation. These forms make feasible considerable increases of efficacy of value-added chains, de-block, *lock-out*, increase, and accelerate *innovation* through *shared knowledge*—where ideal "markets" typically fail in face of such complexity.

Finally, such *self-organising structures* typically are facilitated by *middle-range sized* "*platforms*", "*arenas*", or groups. Institutional or "cultural" emergence, thus, typically takes place or is most pronounced in what we theoretically call "*meso*"-economic entities, which *co-evolve* with successful coordination. In other words, succeeding coordination and cooperation require both minimum critical masses of cooperating agents but also the constitution of informal groups of agents *smaller* than whole large anonymous populations. This is why we talk of empirical phenomena such as regional, industrial, cluster or network cultures. In the larger framework of evolutionary-institutional complexity modelling we may talk here of "*meso-economics*". In reality, however, such ideal self-organization structures among independent small and medium-sized firms are overlaid with the reality of corporate size, power, and oligopoly. Therefore, the global corporate economy reveals combined structures of networks and hierarchy, i.e., so-called *hub&spoke* networks.

Finally, such processes and emerging structures often are *blocked*, or *locked-in* after some time of a historical *institutional life cycle*, or if agents succeeded with institutional emergence, emerging structures often are *fragile*, may fall back into conventional decentralised "market failure", or often these (learning) processes are highly *time-consuming*.

Coordination and cooperation among private agents then may be *de-blocked* and *initiated, stabilised* or *accelerated* by a modern conception of "*structural*" *economic policy*, that itself interacts with the system of interaction of the private agents, which does not fully substitute the private coordinated action lacking (as in conventional collective-good theory) but influences *incentives* and *expectations* of the private agents in order to improve the conditions of their social learning of coordination/cooperation, resulting in some *"structural" improvement* and, finally, some *common economic advancement*. This can be shown to be a rather lean, "qualitative" economic policy, working with little pecuniary subsidies. We call it *interactive* economic ("structural") *policy*.

This series, basically, is designed to contribute to the different aspects, areas, and questions mentioned of *modern "interactive" meso-economics*. Conventional *microeconomics* appears highly insufficient against the background indicated, and *macroeconomics* still needs reliable "micro-foundations", which will need to be *micro-* and *"meso"-foundations*. In terms of policy, there are manifold and ubiquitous *unintended "structural" consequences* of spontaneous both micro and macro processes, and of conventional both micro- and macro policies. The remedies are supposed to lie in more adequate, theoretically better informed, and well-designed structures of private-private and private-public interactions, at micro, "meso", and macro levels.

Wolfram Elsner, University of Bremen, Germany

Vorwort des Reihenherausgebers

Eines der größeren Themen der Wirtschaftsstruktur- und der Regionalforschung im letzten Jahrzehnt war, im Anschluss an R. Florida (2002 ff.), die Frage der Wirkungen der "kreativen Klasse" auf die Wirtschaftsentwicklung im Allgemeinen und v.a. auf die differentielle Regionalentwicklung. Die Konzepte der "Kreativität" und der "kreativen" Beschäftigten sind offensichtlich recht "fuzzy", wie auch der Autor der vorliegenden Untersuchung schon im Titel bemerkt. Sie sind aber zugleich in der veränderten Welt der "Informationsgesellschaft" (ein nicht minder multivalenter Begriff), unabhängig von Richard Floridas Initialzündung, zu einem relevanten Untersuchungsgegenstand geworden — und haben nicht zuletzt recht schnell den Zugang zu höchst offizieller politischer Aktivität gefunden, wie z.B. die "Initiative Kultur- und Kreativwirtschaft" der Bundesregierung, gestartet bereits im Jahre 2007, belegt. Aber z.B. auch die Statistischen Ämter, Wirtschaftsministerkonferenzen, die EU-Kommission, die Bundesagentur für Arbeit sowie ihr Institut für Arbeitsmarkt- und Berufsforschung (IAB) befassen sich seit längerem mit der Verbesserung der statistischen Grundlagen, mit empirischen Studien sowie mit politischen Fördermöglichkeiten dieser neuen "Querschnittsbranche". Insgesamt also widmet sich der vorliegende Band einem analytisch vielversprechenden, relevanten und zudem sehr aktuellen und politikträchtigen Thema.

Nachdem es für die USA und andere Länder im Anschluss an R. Florida bereits hochkarätige Folgeuntersuchungen mit entsprechenden konzeptionellen, begrifflichen, empirischen und statistisch-methodischen Klärungen und Verfeinerungen gab (u.a. von E.L. Glaeser, M.S. Gertler u.v.a.; für die Niederlande z.B. P. Nijkamp u.a.), und erste empirische und methodische Studien auch für Deutschland vorgelegt wurden (für das IAB z.B.: Möller/Tubadji 2009), liegt es nahe, Deutschlands "Kreativsektor", v.a. im Vergleich der deutschen Städte und Regionen, weiter zu untersuchen, um dabei Konzepte, Begriffe und Hypothesen noch einmal zu schärfen, die Fragestellung auf theoretisch, analytisch und empirisch-statistisch Machbares zu verfeinern und dann weiteren empirischen Tests zugänglich zu machen. Das ist das Anliegen des vorliegenden Bandes.

Dabei ist das Feld im Grundsatz nicht völlig neu. Der "Querschnittssektor" "Kreativwirtschaft" ist sowohl in der Industrie- wie in der Berufsordnungsstatistik schon früher

nicht völlig unzugänglich gewesen. In der ökonomischen Theorie entsprang die "Ökono-
mik des Kreativen" der lang und breit analysierten Humankapital-Theorie. Und dass
hochwertiges Humankapital besonders ungleich über den Raum verteilt ist, das heißt,
in komplexitätsökonomischer Betrachtung, kritische räumliche Agglomerationsgrade für
eine kritische Dichte der Interaktionsprozesse braucht und insofern v.a. in großen Städten
repräsentiert ist, ist in den Feldern der Informations- und Innovationsökonomik, der
Regional- und Stadtökonomik sowie der Cluster- und Netzwerkökonomik seit langem
bekannt. Hier verortet sich der vorliegende Band.

Die Arbeit fragt nach dem Einfluss der "kreativen Beschäftigten" (1) auf das gesamte
Beschäftigungswachstum und (2) auf das weitere Beschäftigungswachstum der "Kreati-
ven" selbst (im Sinne eines selbstverstärkenden Prozesses) in einer Region. Regionale
Basis sind dabei die 74 Planungsregionen in Deutschland im Zeitraum 1977 bis 2004.

Folgende Forschungsfragen werden gestellt: (1) Wie groß ist die Wirkung des "kreativen
Sektors" auf das Beschäftigungswachstum? (2) Wie groß ist der ökonomische Effekt der
Diversität (der Beschäftigten) (auf das Beschäftigungswachstum)? (3) Gibt es einen
selbstverstärkenden Prozess der "kreativen Beschäftigung" (in einer Region)? (4) Wie
ist die regionale Verteilung der "kreativen Beschäftigung"? (5) Sind Städte Orte mit
einem höheren Anteil "kreativer Beschäftigung" (als andere Regionen)? Und: (6) Welche
(städtischen?) Politikinstrumente sind geeignet, die "kreative Beschäftigung" zu erhöhen?

Der Band beinhaltet eine Literaturauswertung zu den Themenkomplexen, die in Floridas
Hypothesen eine Rolle spielen: "Kreativität"/"Talent", "Diversität"/"Toleranz", sowie
"Technology"/"Wissens-Spillovers"/"regionale Innovationsintensität". Die wichtigsten
Einzelstudien für verschiedene Länder (USA, Schweden, Dänemark, Deutschland) werden
im Einzelnen sowie vergleichend vorgestellt, und ihre Schwachpunkte herausgearbeitet.
Die Arbeit lehnt sich dann an einen Modelltyp von J. Suedekum (2006, 2008) an, der auf
einem Humankapital-Ansatz basiert.

Der eigene theoretische Ansatz beginnt mit der Unterscheidung von "kreativer" und
"nicht-kreativer" Beschäftigung mit dem Ziel, die "kreative Beschäftigung" genauer zu
bestimmen. Es folgt ein formales Modell einer "kreativen Stadt", ein regionalökono-
mischer Ansatz. Das Modell veranschaulicht, (1) dass der Lohnsatz der "weniger Kreativen" mit dem Anteil der "Kreativen" in der Region (Stadt) steigt, während (2) der Lohnsatz der "Kreativen" selbst entsprechend sinkt. Der allgemeine Technologie- (Produk-
tivitäts-) Parameter wird sodann sowohl vom Anteil der "Kreativen" an der regionalen
Gesamtbeschäftigung (moduliert mit einem Faktor der Humankapital-Externalitäten) als
auch von einem komplexen Faktor der lokalen Lebensqualität ("local amenities") abhängig
gemacht. Es kann nach Umformungen abgeleitet werden, dass der Lohnsatz der "Kreati-

ven" negativ vom ihrem Beschäftigtenanteil (s.o.), aber positiv vom Grad der Spillovers abhängt während der Lohnsatz der "weniger Kreativen" umgekehrt abhängig ist. "Kreative" werden daher umso eher von einer Stadt angezogen, eine Stadt ist also umso attraktiver für "Kreative", je geringer (höher) ihr bisheriger Anteil (Lohnsatz), aber auch je höher der Spillover-Effekt (und damit ihr Lohnsatz) ist. Damit kann zugleich illustriert werden, dass bei Abwesenheit von Spillover-Mechanismen in einer Lokalität die Anteile der "Kreativen" zwischen den Städten konvergieren würden und dass v.a. die Intensität der Externalitäten und der ihnen zugrundliegenden Interdependenzen und Mechanismen sowie der resultierenden kumulativen, pfadabhängigen Interaktionsprozesse die regionalen Divergenzen des Anteils der "Kreativen" erklären können eine Erkenntnis, die gut in den größeren Kontext komplexer kumulativer raumbezogener Ökonomik gestellt werden kann.

Die lokalen "Annehmlichkeiten" werden durch den Anteil der Bohemiens operationalisiert, und der Einfluss dieser für die 'Kreativen' (gemäß Florida) wichtigen Dimension von "Lebensqualität" wird empirisch geschätzt. Das Gleiche gilt für den Einfluss der Diversität, der bereits bei Florida das Potential der regionalen Lerneffekte indiziert.

Es werden folgende Haupt-Hypothesen entwickelt: (1) Das gesamte Beschäftigungswachstum einer Region ist eine positive Funktion des lokalen Anteils der "Kreativen", die sich aus den lokalen "kreativen Professionals" und den lokalen "Bohemiens" zusammensetzen (Bezug Forschungsfrage 1). (2) Das gesamte Beschäftigungswachstum einer Region ist eine po-sitive Funktion der lokalen Diversität, die sich aus der lokalen Diversität der "Professionals" und der lokalen allgemeinen "ethnisch-kulturellen Diversität" (gemessen mit einem inversen Herfindahl-Hirschman Index) zusammensetzt (Bezug Forschungsfrage 2). (3) Die Wachstumsrate der Beschäftigung der "kreativen Professionals" ist eine Funktion des Anteils der "kreativen Professionals" (Bezug Forschungsfrage 3). (4) Die Wachstumsrate der Beschäftigung der "kreativen Professionals" ist eine Funktion des Anteils der Bohemiens (Bezug Forschungsfrage 3). (5) Der "kreative Sektor" ist in Deutschland regional relativ ungleich verteilt (Bezug Forschungsfrage 4). (6) Die "kreativen Professionals" sind in den großen Agglomerationen konzentriert (Bezug Forschungsfrage 5).

Die datenmäßig und statistisch exakten Definitionen von "kreativen Professionals", alternativ als "kreativer Sektor" (mit "technisch-kultureller" Kreativität) und als "kreative Klasse" (mit technischer, kultureller und ökonomischer Kreativität), sowie von "hochqualifizierten Beschäftigten" ("high-skilled agents", konkret als Beschäftigte mit Universitätsabschluss) sind in der Arbeit ausgewiesen. Nach Datenbeschreibung und -aufbereitung, weiter spezifizierter datenbezogener Variablendefinition, Darlegung der summarischen statistischen Eigenschaften des Datensatzes und Formulierung der zu erwartenden Vor-zeichen von Regressionskoeffizienten, erfolgt die Ermittlung der regionalen Verteilung der "kreativen Professionals" und ihrer Entwicklung. Es folgt eine Spezifikation einer ökono-metrischen Gleichung (für alternative Konzepte und Variablendefinitionen). Die Datenstruktur (insbes. die unterschiedliche jährliche Verfügbarkeit der unabhängigen und abhän-gigen Variablen) lassen i. W. eine Lag-Struktur von drei Jahren in allen ökonometrischen Gleichungen angemessen erscheinen.

Die Regressionsergebnisse bestätigen i. W. die Hypothesen über die Einflüsse auf das allgemeine regionale Beschäftigungswachstum für die "kreativen Professionals", konkre-tisiert als "technologierelevant Beschäftigte", mit den Alternativen "kreativer Sektor" und "krea-tive Klasse", sowie als "hochqualifizierte Beschäftigte". Die Bestandsgröße des "kreativen Sektors" wirkt aber oft auch negativ auf dessen weiteres Größenwachstum. Auch die Wirkung der Bohemiens ist nicht durchgängig positiv. Einige Ergebnisse vari-ieren zwischen den alternativ verwendeten Variablen bzw. Konzepten.

Der "kreative Sektor" und seine Diversität haben insgesamt jedoch überwiegend einen deutlich positiven Einfluss auf das gesamte Beschäftigungswachstum, und er unterliegt zugleich einem selbst-verstärkenden Prozess in Bezug auf sich selbst. Dies gilt aber v.a. für große Agglomerationen, die die entsprechenden selbstverstärkenden Konzen-trationsprozesse (über vermutete Wissens-Spillovers) mobilisieren können. Regionen mit geringeren Anteilen an "Kreativen" fallen eher zurück und konvergieren mit dem Regionen-Mittelwert. Die regionale Divergenz findet also zwischen den "Top-Regionen" und allen anderen Regionen statt.

Einige Policy-Implikationen scheinen auf der Hand zu liegen: "kreative Professionals" anziehen, Diversifizierung fördern sowie lokale Netzwerke mit "knowledge sharing" und "knowledge spillovers" fördern. Wie das aber im Einzelnen gehen kann, und v.a. wie es im Zweifel in einer mittelgroßen Stadt oder Agglomeration bei noch nicht vorhandener kumulativer Selbstverstärkung erfolgreich durchgeführt werden könnte, wäre im Rahmen weiterer komplexitätstheoretisch bzw. evolutionsökonomisch angelegter Untersuchungen zu analysieren.

Eine vergleichende statistische Untersuchung zu den drei größten Städten Deutschlands sowie eine Policy-orientierte Case Study zu Hamburg rundet das Bild ab. Hamburg "schwimmt" bekanntermaßen auf dem Trend zur Selbstverstärkung des "kreativen Sek-tors" der in dieser Hinsicht kleinen Zahl von "Top-Städten". Viele praktische Maßnahmen müssen daher nur eine gewisse Verstärkung eines ohnehin stattfindenden Prozesses sein.

Insgesamt wird damit ein neue Erkenntnisse generierender Beitrag zur aktuellen Ökono-mik der "Kreativität", "kreativer Sektoren" und "kreativer Städte" vorgelegt. Ein inte-ressantes und weitreichendes Netz von alternativen Konzepten, Begriffen und Variablen wurde hier untersucht, und der weitere Diskurs in diesem Forschungsfeld wird sich auf das Spektrum dieser Ergebnisse beziehen müssen. Der theoretische Bezug zur Ökonomik komplexer bzw. evolutorischer Prozesse ist dabei offensichtlich, parallel zum laufenden ökonomisch-sozialwissenschaftlichen Diskurs zu Interaktionsprozessen und emergenten Strukturen, einschließlich der komplexen Konzepte "Vertrauen" und "Reziprozität" bzw. informelle Institutionen. Netzwerke und sog. Sozialkapital.

Bremen. April 2012 W. Elsner.

Geleitwort

Seit Richard Florida (2002) wird die Bedeutung der "kreativen Klasse" für die Entwicklung von Volkswirtschaften und Regionen diskutiert. Dabei stellt sich die Frage, ob und inwieweit die Förderung von Kunst und Kultur einen positiven Einfluss auf die wirtschaftliche Entwicklung einer Region hat. Die hohe Relevanz dieser wirtschaftspolitischen Debatte aus der sich auch die umfangreiche Initiative zur Kultur- und Kreativwirtschaft der Bundesregierung ergeben hat steht in einem krassen Wiederspruch zur bisherigen theoretischen und empirischen Fundierung des Konzepts der kreativen Klasse.

Diese Lücke wird zumindest in wichtigen Teilen durch die Dissertation von Herrn Jan Wedemeier gefüllt. Er untersucht zum einen, wie sich die kreative Klasse auf das Beschäftigungswachstum insgesamt auswirkt, zum anderen in welchem Zusammenhang die Beschäftigung in der kreativen Klasse auf das weitere Wachstum der "Kreativen" selbst (im Sinne eines selbstverstärkenden Prozesses) steht. Regionale Basis sind dabei zunächst eine (abstrakte) Volkswirtschaft insgesamt, sodann aber die konkreten 74 Raum-ordnungsregionen in Deutschland im Zeitraum 1977 bis 2004.

Für die empirische Untersuchung werden Variablen wie "kreativ Beschäftigte", "kreativer Sektor" und "kreative Klasse" sowie hochqualifizierte Beschäftigte eingeführt und statistisch abgegrenzt, und in der Literatur oft diffuse Variablen wie lokale "Annehmlichkeiten" werden zu "Bohemiens" operationalisiert. So kann der Einfluss dieser für die "Kreativen" wichtigen Dimension von "Annehmlichkeiten" geschätzt werden.

Das Gleiche gilt für den Einfluss der Diversität, der bereits bei Florida das Potenzial der regionalen Lerneffekte indiziert. Die Ergebnisse zeigen, dass der "kreative Sektor" und dessen Diversität einen positiven Effekt auf das gesamte Beschäftigungswachstum haben. Außerdem gibt es einen sich selbst-verstärkenden Prozess bei der kreativen Beschäftigung. Dies tritt besonders bei großen Agglomerationen auf. Regionen mit geringeren Anteilen an "Kreativen" fallen gegenüber solchen mit einem hohen Anteil zurück.

Insofern führen die empirischen Untersuchungen zu neuen Erkenntnissen über die Bedeutung der "Kreativität", aus denen sich wiederum neue interessante Fragenstellungen, auch für die Wirtschaftspolitik, ergeben.

Hamburg, April 2012 Michael Bräuninger

Acknowledgments

Scores of people supported me with this book and I shall never completely be able to acknowledge all of them.

In particular, I would like to express my gratitude to participants of the 7th European Urban and Regional Studies (EURS) Conference which was held in Istanbul, Turkey, in 2008. At that conference, I presented some preliminary results of my PhD project in a special session on "Diversity and the Creative Capacity of Cities and Regions". Prof. Dr. Peter Nijkamp (Vrije Universiteit Amsterdam (VU), the Netherlands), Prof. Dr. Tüzin Baycan Levent (Istanbul Technical University, Turkey), Dr. Giovanni Prarolo (Fondazione Eni Enrico Mattei (FEEM), Milan, and University of Bologna, Italy) and others participated at that special session and their comments and suggest improvements for my work were a great help. As a result, in 2009 a paper was published in the Journal of European Planning Studies. I am also grateful to the unknown referees for their helpful ideas and suggestions.

Second, in 2008 I participated at the summer school of the 4th Urban Research in Europe Conference (FUTURE) which was held in Weimar, Germany. It was an international summer school on urban economics and the ethnically diverse city. Later in 2008, I presented a paper at the FUTURE Conference reviewing on theories and empirical studies relevant for the concept of diversity of economic agents and the creative cities literature. This paper is published as a working paper and in a chapter of a book by Prof. Dr. Eckardt (University Weimar, Germany) and Prof. Dr. John Eade (Roehampton University, London, UK).

In 2008 and 2009, I attended and presented some of my working results at the 48th and 49th European Congress of the Regional Science Association International (ERSA) in Liverpool (UK) and Lodz (Poland). There I received helpful comments and suggestions from different persons, but especially from Dr. Katja Wolf from the Institute for Employment Research (IAB, Germany), Dr. Ugo Fratesi (Politechnico di Milano, Italy), and Dr. Stephan Brunow (Technische Universität Dresden, Germany).

Fourth, I would like to thank FEEM, who hosted me in 2009. In Milan I worked on the topic of "Knowledge Creation, Creativity and Diversity in Cities", together with Dr. Cristina Catteno (FEEM), Dr. Giovanni Prarolo (FEEM, and University of Bologna), and Dr. Max Steinhardt (Hamburg Institute of International Economics, HWWI, Germany). The project was co-financed by a scholarship from the European Commission within the framework of the "SUS.DIV Training Exchange Programme". In Milan, I was able to develop my technical skills regarding econometric problems and solutions, which was helpful for this work.

I would further like to thank the Bremen University of Applied Sciences for offering the opportunity on multiple occasions to present working results, but particularly in 2010 when I was able to present preliminary results of my PhD thesis at the Pune Summer School. The course supervisor was Prof. Dr. Niemeier (Bremen University of Applied Sciences, Germany).

In 2010, at the University of Bremen, I presented some preliminary problems and solutions from this work. I would especially like to thank seminar participants of the research colloquium at the University of Bremen for their helpful comments, among others Prof. Dr. Christian Cordes, Prof. Dr. Stefan Traub, and Prof. Dr. Wolfram Elsner (all University of Bremen).

More importantly, Prof. Elsner is the first supervisor for the thesis at hand. I would especially like to express my deep gratitude to Prof. Elsner for his willingness to serve in this function. I owe him a great debt for his helpful ideas, comments, and suggestions. His expertise has been very valuable to me and my work.

My gratitude also goes to members of the HWWI - especially to Prof. Dr. Thomas Straubhaar, Prof. Dr. Michael Bräuninger, Dr. Silvia Stiller and to participants of the HWWI PhD seminar - for their advice and comments. Prof. Dr. Bräuninger is the second supervisor for the thesis, and my special thanks go to him as well.

Last, but not least, I would like to thank my partner Insa Balssen for her patience and encouragement, without which I could have never completed this thesis.

Contents

List of Tables

List of Figures

1. Introduction

Explanations for the competitiveness of regions are manifold. A central reason for the competitiveness is their ability to attract and hold high-skilled agents and creative professionals. A sophisticated and excellent regional skill structure is frequently regarded as a major condition for regional employment growth and economic welfare. In particular, creative professionals - that is, economic agents working in the fields of education, engineering, science, and arts - are supposed to be attracted to the places that are the most beneficial to creative and innovative activities (see Florida 2002; Wojan et al. 2007). Moreover, today the most successful places seem to be particularly concentrated in idea-producing industries (see Glaeser 2008). The distribution of such places is unequal in space, which is one explanation for regional economic imbalances.

Whether cultural amenities explain the unequal regional distribution of economic agents is *inter alia* investigated by Falck et al. (2009), Möller and Tubadji (2009), Shaprio (2006), and Wojan et al. (2007). Some of these authors conclude that local cultural amenities support regional evolution and help to explain regional growth disparities. By using an adjusted Roback (1982) model, Shaprio (2006) finds that around 60 percent of employment growth is affected by productivity growth, and the rest is explained by cultural amenities. Möller and Tubadji (2009) follow the hypothesis that a concentration of bohemians results in a higher concentration of creative agents. In contrast to Shaprio (2006), their findings for 323 German regions show no supportive results for this hypothesis. However, more classical conditions affecting economic agent's location decision mechanism are regional capital endowments or the rental costs of housing (see Glaeser 2008).

In cities, people and firms are especially considered as very successful in developing ideas, inventions and innovations. To understand this is to bring up one fundamental definition of cities which is "the absence of physical space between people and firms" (Glaeser 2008, 6). Glaeser - but also others - explain this success through the interaction between economic agents in close proximity, which helps to stimulate the flow of ideas and knowledge between agents (i.e. agglomeration economies). The diverse composition of local economic agents is moreover regarded as a factor in the growth of cities. The main argument is that cities bring together diverse agents in close proximity, thereby fostering the combination and generating of new knowledge (Jacobs 1969; Florida 2002).

However, a pre-requisite for the generation of innovation and economic growth is the regional endowment of economic agents, i.e. human capital. According to Lucas (1988) knowledge spillovers, generated by formal and informal interaction between people, are a possible explanation for persisting economic differences between regions. Lucas argues that especially economic agents working in the fields of "arts and sciences - the creative professions" exchange specific ideas (i.e. the effects of external human capital is common to the arts and sciences) (Lucas 1988, 38). Moreover, he points out the importance of cities in the knowledge transfer, since cities facilitate the accumulation of knowledge transfers and much of economics in cities are "creative", as arts or sciences are.

Those arguments supports Florida's (2002) assumption about the importance of agents working in the creative professions. His research question on the creative sector originates from the insights of the economics of human capital. Florida argues that the economic success and competitive advantages of both cities and regions is based on these creative professionals. They can foster creative processes, ending in innovation and regional employment growth. He further suggests that the regional abundance of creative professionals affects the employment growth of that specific group of professions (i.e. self-reinforcing process). There are studies investigating this effect of human capital, but not on creative professionals. Suedekum (2006; 2008), for example, finds that the share of high-skilled employment has a positive effect on low- and medium-skilled employment growth, but not on employment growth of the high-skilled. Because of the latter results, he concludes that skill complementarities are more important than knowledge spillovers, i.e. that high local spillovers may positively effect the employment growth of the high-skilled agents. Moretti (2004) finds both, spillovers and skill complementarities to be important for employment growth.

The primary motivation of this work derived from Florida's (2002) assumption that creative professions play a crucial role on employment growth. The research focus, however, lies on German regions, since analyses of regional employment growth by creative professionals are still scarce and especially empirical evidence is lacking.

Generally, there are a number of reasons why this research is important. First, the theory used in the current economic literature on the creative sector is not well-formulated. On the topic of the creative sector, most economists tend to start with the data and empiricism, but understanding the creative sector also requires a scientific theory. Second, there are few empirical works for Germany, especially on the effects of the creative sector on total employment, but, there are neither theoretical nor empirical analyses on the creative sector employment growth self, i.e. self-reinforcing process. Third, the link between the diversity of economic agents and the creative sector - which is widely discussed in the literature on the creative sector, but empirical evidence is still scarce - is followed as well in the thesis at hand. Here, the diversity of creative professionals and the ethnic-cultural diversity of economic agents is analysed, since it is assumed that both stimulate employment growth, because of their potential to increase the rate of interchange between different ideas and knowledge.

The work addresses all three points, and the empirical results show that the creative sector fosters regional employment growth, whereas it contributes further to the regional concentration of that specific employment group. Moreover, diversity is further important for employment growth.

1.1. Contribution and content

Contribution. The overall research objective is to contribute to the question of whether the economic factor of creativity, i.e. the creative sector, has an impact on regional employment growth in German regions. This research question can be traced back to Richard Florida's (2002) bestseller *The rise of the creative class and how it's transforming work, leisure, community, and everyday life*, which has become one of the "hot" topics in regional and city planning. Florida's (2002) book induced several studies covering the research question of whether the creative sector has an impact on the real economy, but most studies simply present the regional distribution of the creative sector. Furthermore, what is completely lacking in the current literature about the creative sector is a well formulated theory. Consequently, the book at hand provides novel empirical evidence on the economic impact of the creative sector on employment growth based on a well-formulated methodology and theory. Thus, the work will consider the following important research questions:

1. How important is the creative sector for employment growth?

2. How relevant are the economic effects originating from the diversity (of employment) on employment growth?

3. Is there a self-reinforcing process of pooled creative professionals?

4. What does the regional distribution of creative professionals look like?

5. (a) Are cities places with a higher share of creative professionals,

   (b) and what (urban) policy instruments strengthen creative sector employment?

Research questions one through five are developed in the following chapters and narrowed down in chapter 4, on the work's hypotheses and research design.

In its results, this work will report new, hitherto unknown results, as the scientific research is new in the context of its ideas, methodology and presentation. The analysis of creative professionals, and diversity is mainly related to two current topics in regional economics, namely the economies of human capital and its effects on regional employment growth and the topic of the creative economy.

Content. The remaining chapters of the book are organised as follows. Chapter 2, the literature review, discusses the current literature on the topic of the creative sector. It is an intellectual starting point for this work and records the main, as well as current, economic literature in the field. First, the second chapter provides an answer to the question of where the concept of the creative sector comes from. It points out the background knowledge and methodological approaches as well as definitions. Second, the chapter further views on economic literature that captures the effect of the creative sector and the diverse composition of economic agents on (employment) growth. Since the research focuses on the question of the creative economy in Germany, the focal point of the literature review will rely, with some exceptions, on studies of Europe and, in particular, Germany. This limitation helps to understand a number of important features when considering Germany's economic and institutional system with regard to the creative economy. Chapter 2 closes with a critique of methods and contents.

The theoretical framework of the analysis is outlined in chapter 3. It provides a theoretical approach to the fuzzy concept of the creative sector. Before continuing with the empirical study of the problems and importance of the creative sector, a theoretical model is introduced which helps to explain why some economic agents are creative and others not. In section 3.1, this problem is solved by arguing on a human capital model taken from Murphy et al. (1991). It is further recalled that the current economic literature on the study's interest does not provide any theoretical model. Therefore, section 3.2 starts by applying a human capital model built on Moretti (2004), but which mainly follows Suedekum (2006, 2008). First of all, the model helps to understand the relationship between the creative sector and the total employment growth. Moreover, the model's focus lies on the self-reinforcing process of already pooled creative professionals. One of Florida's main assumptions is that high shares of creative professionals will further encourage the accumulation of more creative professionals. However, the theoretical effort will provide an important bridge to the empirical analysis.

Chapter 4 turns to the main and minor hypotheses of the empirical work. In consideration of the explanatory power of this scientific project, the fourth chapter explains the research design of the empirical research to address the five research questions outlined previously. Furthermore, the final working definition of the creative sector is presented. Chapter 5 presents the empirical part of this work, exhibiting results regarding the creative sector's impact on regional employment growth. Chapter 5.1 describes the data. Chapter 5.2 provides a statistical overview of Germany's creative sector. Maps and other statistical material is presented. In chapter 5.3 the econometric model is presented. Using a fixed effects model with time-lags, two different definitions of the creative sector and one skill specific employment definition are applied and investigated. Chapter 5.4 presents the regression results. In order to complete this work, the results' implications are discussed in chapter 6. Moreover, in the sixth chapter the general conclusions from the empirical insights are highlighted.

The seventh chapter presents a case study from the city of Hamburg. For Hamburg, new data are presented. However, this chapter deals with policy instruments adequate for supporting the creative sector. It is important to bring policy into the debate of creative cities, because it makes scientific disciplines and also this research work useful. In the final chapter the findings are highlighted. At first, a summary of all chapters is presented. Second, chapter 8 points out the limitations of the work at hand and raises questions which might be addressed in future research. Finally, the thesis will conclude with remarks on the lessons that can be drawn from the work.

This thesis is further organised into four parts. Figure 1.1. illustrates this organisation.

Figure 1.1.: Organisation of the dissertation

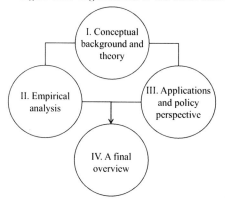

This didactic has been chosen, since different data and definitions for reasons of actuality and political relevance are applied. The first part concerns the conceptual background and theory of the thesis topic of the creative sector. It contains chapter 2, which is the literature review, and chapter 3, the theoretical framework. The second part pertains to empiricism and is comprised of chapter 4, the hypotheses, chapter 5, the empirical section of this thesis, and finally the implications and conclusions to be drawn from the empirical study, in chapter 6. In order to complete this effort, part III consists of applications and policy perspectives for the creative sector. That chapter contains actual data and is notionally separated from part II. This approach is crucial to establishing a clear structure and ordering the definitions and data. This shall guide economic reseachers, readers from politics and other organisations through the thesis. The last section, part IV, is the final overview and contains the eighth chapter, the conclusion.

Part I.

Conceptual background and theory

2. Review on creative cities and regions

In order to facilitate a better understanding of the research questions and develop the hypotheses, this work begins with the literature review. Section 2.1 offers a review on the origin of research related to the creative sector. Section 2.2 shows the current state of research on the creative sector. It presents some methods in the economic literature, which have looked at the creative sector and economic as well as employment growth.

This review focuses on economic research for Europe and, in particular, Germany. This shall help frame the empirical case of the employment and creative professionals' growth in Germany presented in chapter 5. Besides focusing on the creative sector, the review at hand further show the link between the creative sector and diversity. Section 2.3 closes with a critique of methods and contents. Outlined in the last section of chapter 2, the critique is linked to a number of consequences relevant for the following chapters.

2.1. Talent, tolerance and technology: Stylised facts on creativity

Florida (2002) argues that so-called creative professionals contribute to explaining economic transformation and growth. Florida's hypothesis is that these professionals are marked by capabilities and skills which foster structural transformation towards a knowledge-based and creative economy. Therefore, the creative professionals are supposed to be the main drivers of cities' and regions' knowledge-based economies.

Florida's (2002) basic argument is that the economic success and competitive advantage of cities and regions is based on talent, technology and tolerance. The assumption is that these three locational factors attract professionals of the creative sector. The implication of these three factors is that there is a self-reinforcing effect generated, meaning the local structure and endowment of these three factors is also regarded as a major cause for economic growth disparities. Florida's (2002) assumption is that the results of this self-reinforcing effect takes place especially in cities, due to the fact that they have an advantage in educating and keeping those economic agents who play a major role in the (creative) economy.[1] Most important, cities also have the ability to attract, and advantage that they can attract economic agents. This polarisation of agents at one place affects productivity through knowledge spillovers which are seen as a crucial factor for economic growth (for a further discussion on knowledge spillovers, see, for example, Lucas 1988; Marshall 1920a; Porter 1998).

Spillovers of knowledge are facilitated by face-to-face contacts. Due to the fact that cities are confronted by the absence of physical space between individual agents, firms, or (formal) institutions, face-to-face contacts occur more often in cities, and therefore transaction costs are regarded as being lower in cities than in rural areas (Glaeser 2008).[2]

Since Florida (2002; 2003; 2005; 2009) is the main driver behind the concept and idea of creativity and creative cities, the following short introduction highlights the insights of his book *The rise of the creative class and how it's transforming work, leisure, community, and everyday life*. Understanding the urban geography of creativity and its effects on economic outcomes lies in what Florida calls the "creativity index" which captures the extent of the three locational conditions of talent, technology and tolerance within a region. These three factors are interdependent locational conditions and, therefore, each measure alone is assumed to be insufficient for stimulating economic growth. In following, this three locational factors are briefly explained.

Talent. Talent is captured by the variable for the creative sector. In the economic literature talent generally covers economic agents with high-skilled competence, a high educational level or special competence (see, for instance, Murphy et al. 1991; Wojan et al. 2007). In the literature on the creative sector, talent signifies the share of the economic agents working as creative professionals. Florida (2002) divides the creative sector into the two sub groups, a "(super) creative core" as well as "creative professionals" and distinguishes them from the industrial sector, the service sector, and the agricultural sector. The "(super) creative core" agents work in the fields of computing, mathematics, architecture, education, training, arts, design, sports and others. In these professions agents are paid to be visionary, to develop new ideas and invent new approaches. "Creative professionals" are occupied or self-employed in business and financial operations, management, law, health care, high-end sales, sales management, as well as other areas.

---

1 Thereby, cities have the advantage of being locations within the system of universities. Universities contribute to the economy, since university cities will remain well-educated economic agents with the ability for abstract thinking and learning. For further discussion, see, *inter alia*, Glaeser (1994), Lundvall (2002), or Shaprio (2006).
2 For the discussion on transaction costs and institutions, see, for example, Elsner et al. (2010) or Elsner and Heinrich (2009).

These professionals access their large pool of skills, experience and knowledge in order to solve particular problems. Their work is comprised of many routinely performed tasks.[3]

Florida's (2002) concept of the creative sector originates from the economics of human capital (for the discussion on human capital, see, for example, Lucas 1988; Rauch 1993; Romer 1990). Florida chooses to measure human capital in terms of a measure of the creative sector instead of a measure of educational concentration (see, for instance, Marrocu and Paci 2010). The difference is not a region's educational endowment but a region's professional endowment of human capital, which he argues explains economic development. This distinction between educational and professional endowment can be made since human capital refers to the accumulation of productive abilities, experiences or knowledge embodied in agents. That means human capital does not refer to education alone. This definition is different from Becker's (1975) influential human capital definition, which mainly focused on an agent's education.

Florida's (2002) argument is that economic and employment growth depends on innovation and productive processes caused by agents with creative abilities. In other words, he introduces a human capital concept based on occupations which captures proper creative abilities ending in economic growth. As a result, agents of the creative sector are therefore not necessarily a highly educated group of agents (Hansen 2008; Marlet and van Woerkens 2004).[4]

However, Florida's main statistical findings are that the creative sector tends to concentrate in strong economic regions, mostly in cities, with relatively high growth rates. Moreover, he argues - though, he does not provide empirical evidence - that already high shares of creative agents will lead to higher shares of creative agents, in a so-called self-reinforcing process.[5]

Tolerance. Florida (2002) noticed that several empirical studies on urban economics and employment growth point out that economic diversity has a positive impact on economic growth. Thereby, he is heavily influenced by studies from Jane Jacobs (1969) and Jacobs (1992). The urban planer Jacobs argued that cities bring together both diverse economic agents and a variety of regionally proximate industries.[6] This economic diversity - so the

---

3 Appendix A.1.1 gives a detailed overview of Florida's (2002) classification.

4 This difference in the definition might be especially relevant for countries with important vocational education structures such as Germany. The vocational education system is highly relevant in preparing individuals for the labour market in non-academic activities. Moreover, many Anglo-Saxon countries include typical German vocational education and training measures as part of bachelor degree programs.

5 This argument is further to be found in the literature on human capital, which argues that (regions and) cities are stimulated by the size of locational human capital endowments (see, *inter alia*, Glaeser and Saiz 2004; Rauch 1993; Suedekum 2006).

6 Empirical evidence that knowledge spillovers might occur between, rather than within, economic in-

assumption by Jacobs - will help to reduce the risk of lock-in on an inferior technology, also known as innovation failures.[7] and will turn ideas into new businesses. The main argument for this assumption is that the potential for the interchange of diverse knowledge and ideas, but especially the random collisions of businesses, is greater within diverse economic structures (i.e. knowledge spillovers). Diversity stimulates if indirectly, economic growth through this positive externality.[8]

Several empirical findings indicate that cities and regions, which are characterised by a distinct diversity of economic agents by nationality, foster economic growth (Ottaviano and Peri 2004; Niebuhr 2006; Damelang et al. 2007; Bellini et al. 2008). The diversity of economic agents enables this benefit by increasing the variety of production and consumption (Ottaviano and Peri 2004; Bellini et al. 2008). Florida (2002) grasps this theory and goes a step further. His basic assumption for explaining urban economic growth is that economic agents who decide to migrate will be strongly attracted to open and tolerant cities. He highlights that low entry barriers for economic agents are worthwhile, since agents can integrate themselves faster in markets if barriers such as forms of social barriers and arrangements are low. This argument comes from the literature of entrepreneurship, where low barriers of entry for firms are emphasised as factors for promoting new products and competition.

Against this background, Florida primarily uses a variable describing the share of homosexual couples within a region relative to the national average (the "gay index") to measure tolerance and open cities. To further measure locations with low entry barriers, Florida uses a "melting-pot index" accounting for the percentage of foreign-born people in a city. Besides the "melting-pot-index" he also introduces a "bohemian index" which measures the share of bohemians - agents working as artists, musicians or publishers - in a city. The "bohemian index" - and this is different from many later works on the creative economy - is not part of Florida's (2002) creative sector itself. Florida's empirical results show that the share of bohemians is a relatively strong predictor for attracting profes-

---

dustries - the diversity argument - is provided for US Metropolitan Statistical Areas (MSA) by Glaeser et al. (1992). This argument rests on Jacobs' externality. The results show that specialised economies are more linked to mature products, i.e. spatial diversity and specialisation depends on the life cycle of products (Glaeser et al. 1992, for a discussion on this argument, see, for example, Duranton and Puga 2000, Duranton and Puga 2001 or Quigley 1998). This specialisation argument is known as the Marshall-Arrow-Romer (MAR) externality which "concerns knowledge spillovers between firms in a [local monopoly] industry" (Glaeser et al. 1992, 1127). The last argument in regard to the Jacobs and MAR externalities is that localised, competitive and pooled industries with small firms are supposed to foster economic growth (Porter externality). However, Glaeser et al.'s empirical results provide evidence for this argument and it is interpreted as the dynamic benefit of competitiveness among small firms.

7 For the problematic of lock-in processes, see, *inter alia*, David (1985), Elsner (2004, 2005), or Hansen (2008).

8 For an overview on creative cities and the concept of diversity, see, *inter alia*, Wedemeier (2011)

sionals of the creative sector. Furthermore, bohemians are regarded as a factor impacting the creativity of agents.

Neither the "melting-pot index" nor the "bohemian index" are a part of Florida's empirical analysis, but he employs them to support further arguments. He also introduces the "composite-diversity index" which adds together the three measures for locations with low entry and social barriers, the "gay index", "melting-pot index" and "bohemian index". Some of the statistical findings of Florida's work for the Metropolitan Statistical Area (MSA) in the United States indicate that the "composite-diversity index" is positively correlated and significant with the technology variable "high-tech index".

Technology. Nonetheless, Florida regarded the technological state of a region as a key determinant for its economic performance. As an indicator of a region's capability for technological competitiveness, Florida uses Milken Institute's "tech-pole index" which consists of two partial indices measuring a region's relative high-tech industrial output and the region's own economic output from high-tech industries in relation to the national proportion. This can be understood as a relative measure for high-tech clusters.[9]

He further introduces a second indicator measuring the technological capability that is the "innovation index". This index is captured by the variable patents per capita. Studying innovation, which is here defined as the invention brought to market,[10] has previously been incorporated in several other study areas of industrial districts (for further discussion, see, for example, Asheim 1996; Marshall 1920a), regional clusters (for further discussion, see, *inter alia.*Elsner 2000; Maskell and Lorenzen 2004a; Porter 1998) and (regional) innovation systems (for further discussion, see, for example, Cantner 2000; Howells 1999; Lundvall 1992).[11] Florida's (2002) ideas on innovation and its importance for economic growth originate from the literature on innovations and regions.

Table 2.1 offers a summary of the locational factors talent, tolerance, and technology, which make up Florida's creativity index.

---

9 Clusters can be defined as regionally concentrated "groups of firms which are functionally interconnected" (Elsner 2000, 413). Clusters establish stable interactions between economic agents and in this way more stable expectations, i.e. a form of trust (contingent trust), which is regarded as important in an innovation process. For a definition and discussion of clusters, see, *inter alia*, Elsner (2000, 2004, 2005), or Porter (1998).

10 An innovation is a commercialised idea or an invention brought to market. An invention is a new composition (incremental), product, process and is based on pre-existing or new knowledge. Knowledge which is not commercialised by a firm generates new opportunities for entrepreneurship which in turn effects economic growth in terms of production and income (see Acs et al. 2004; Schumpeter 1950).

11 An innovation is the result of a creative process, which is systematic or non-systematic. Since many innovations are systematic, the object of the research on innovation systems is to investigate the interaction in the production, diffusion and economic use of knowledge (Lundvall 1992).

Table 2.1.: Florida's creativity index for locational competitiveness

Measure	Index/Variable	Definition
Talent	Creative sector	Region's share of super-creative core and creative professionals
Tolerance	Gay	Measure of the over- or under-representation of coupled gay people
Technology	High-tech	Metropolitan regions high-tech industrial output as a percentage of total US high-tech industrial output; percentage of region's own total economic output that comes from high-tech industries in relation to nationwide percentage
	Innovation	Region's share of patented inventions per capita

Source: Florida (2002, 334).

The main critique of Florida's (2002) research focuses on its methodology, since he mostly simply ranks results. A further critique is if the above highlighted variables for the attraction of agents in the creative sector are really important factors in decisions about location as made by these professionals, or just simply location conditions necessary for all agents of the knowledge economy. Moreover, as further methodology Florida runs several cross-sectional analysis to find correlations between the different indices and variables, but there is a lack of clear documentation and reporting. One example is that Florida provides no documentation either on tests for robustness nor on clear strategies for avoiding endogeneity bias to provide strong evidence for his main hypotheses that the creative sector forces regional growth. The data sources used are also not well-documented (see also Glaeser 2005). Furthermore, Florida (2002) supports his basic thesis with qualitative research methods, i.e. interviews. However, the interview techniques and questions, sample size, and results are simply not reported. The interview results are instead documented haphazardly by way of well-written anecdotes. In section 2.3, more fundamental criticisms are discussed.

2.2. Further literature on creative professionals

In the further economic literature on creative cities, creativity is broadly defined as a factor possibly explaining growth in terms of employment, production and income.[12]

---

12 Creativity here, however, is not defined as a concept of urban planning or "creativity planning", where creativity is understood as a novel method or "toolkit" for strategic, projected urban planning (see,

There are three different types of creativity: First, creativity is linked to Schumpeterian creative destruction which describes the transformation of one economy into another through technological progress (Schumpeter 1950; Florida 2002). This process is defined as technological creativity in the context of innovation and growth. It is regarded as a pre-condition for invention. Secondly, creativity is linked to cultural creativity. This type of creativity is used in the context of, for instance, literary, artistic, or musical content. Thirdly, creativity is linked to management and the competency to lead or organise production. This is called economic creativity. The content of creativity always implicates a creative process for products, income, or businesses.[13]

This definition necessarily implies that creativity is not an exclusive form of a cultural (or artistic) concept, albeit in the literature the term is often linked to the concept of "cultural industries" (von Osten 2008) or to the 2009 German definition of "Cultural and Creative Economy" (*Kultur- und Kreativwirtschaft*) (Wirtschaftsministerkonferenz 2009; Söndermann et al. 2009; Söndermann 2009). In this work culture, or cultural amenities, is defined as a location factor for the attractiveness of cities or regions and is simultaneously an economic product.[14] Economic agents working in the field of culturally related professions are bohemians, they are supposed to create new products, to have an effect on taste, and to give an impulse to production.[15] In this thesis, bohemians are an integrated part of the creative sector.

Creativity is often linked - as discussed above - to a statistical definition by sector or occupation. Recall that in the same way, the concept is frequently associated with the term creative cities. The latter describes the socio-economic relevance of urban development in the context of the creative sector with its influencing factors and effects of changing locational conditions (i.e. talent, tolerance, and technology).

---

for instance, Liebmann and Robischon 2003; Landry 2006). In "creativity planning" the key message is to give "confidence that creative and innovative solutions to urban problems are feasible" (Landry 2006, preface), in place of an old intellectual apparatus or bureaucratic mindset. Landry (2006) coined the term of the creative city in the 1990s, the hallmark of which is the ability to adapt to new market conditions in order to solve problems of all kinds. Florida (2002) justifies the importance of this aspect arguing that creativity is the ability of agents to create new knowledge and to deploy existing knowledge. The main shift is the focus on agents ability and not only on (formal) institutional ability (see, for instance, dos Santos-Duisenberg et al. 2008). Moreover, creativity here is also not understood, as in many economic debates, as a marketing strategy for cities which is adopted to attract firms, people, and to become a "hot" place.

13 With the linkage to production and income, I basically follow the definition, for instance, by Söndermann et al. (2009).

14 For further discussion on the impact of bohemians on economic agents, see, *inter alia*, Falck et al. (2009) or Möller and Tubadji (2009).

15 For further discussion on the role of bohemians, see, for instance, (List 1925)

This economical concept of creativity as applied to cities has been adopted and implemented by urban planners worldwide, especially in the United States (US) and Canada (for more discussion, see, for example, Florida et al. 2008; Gertler et al. 2002; Lee et al. 2004; Wu 2005; Wojan et al. 2007).

The focus of this further section, however, lies on European and, in particular, German studies focusing on the creative sector. This focal point has been chosen because of a high level of interest in recent years, and in order to encourage conclusions for the development of German cities which deal with different conditions than the US or Canadian cities. Several qualitative and quantitative research empirical studies have been published in the context of Europe and the creative sector, such as those by Chantelot et al. (2010) for the creative sector's geography in France, Könönen et al. (2008) for nine Baltic Sea cities, Lorenzen and Andersen (2007) on European cities, Florida and Tinagli (2004) for European countries, Maskell and Lorenzen (2004b) for European furniture and music producers, and Mellander and Florida (2007) for Swedish labour market regions. However, the studies from Andersen and Lorenzen (2005) for Danish cities, Fritsch and Stützer (2006) for German administrative districts, Hansen (2007) for Swedish labour market regions, Kröhnert et al. (2007) for the Federal States of Germany, as well as Möller and Tubadji (2009) on 323 West German regions are in the following presented. These last research studies represent a selection (in alphabetical order) of empirical studies that have adopted Florida's (2002) concept of creativity and which are briefly presented in following.

Andersen and Lorenzen (2005): The Danish case. A "creativity index" - as Florida (2002) uses it - is not created as such by Andersen and Lorenzen (2005). Instead, they map the geography of the creative sector in 38 Danish city regions and 273 Danish municipalities. Their results indicate that the creative sector - which consists of the "(super) creative core", "creative professionals" and "bohemians" - tends to concentrate in major cities and city regions. Copenhagen and Aarhus, Denmark's two biggest cities, have the highest ratio - measured by a location coefficient - of the creative sector in general and of the three sub groups "creative core", "creative professionals" and "bohemians" of all Danish city regions.

The Andersen and Lorenzen (2005) findings indicate that the diversity of economic agents - in the corresponding study measured by the ratio of non-western citizens - is statistically significant as an explanatory variable for the location of the creative sector in Denmark. The creative sector *ceteris paribus* generates regional growth. The diversity variable can be interpreted as a variable for tolerant, open locations. The second openness variable is operationalised as the employment rate among non-western citizens. In a bivariate correlation for this openness variable and the creative sector (exclusive bohemians), it indicates no relation. When tested in a model for the independent variables for tolerance on the dependent variable creative sector, there is a significant correlation with the location of the creative sector. This also means that the creative sector tends to locate where the index for the tolerance variables are high.[16]

The indicators on technology are the share of high-tech employment, growth in high-tech employment and the growth of firm starts-ups. Indicators for regional growth, i.e. population and employment growth, are also applied.

The overall results of Andersen's and Lorenzen's research is that places where the creative sector is concentrated have a tendency for more regional growth than other regions. The results are produced with bivariate correlation models and the presented results show high explanatory values. Moreover, most of the variables are statistically significantly correlated to the location of the creative sector, though the direction of causality is unexplained.

Fritsch and Stützer (2006): Germany's creative sector. Fritsch and Stützer (2006) analyse the creative sector - which also consists of the "(super) creative core", "creative professionals" and "bohemians" - in 439 German districts (Kreise) which include agglomerated, urbanised and rural districts. They investigate where the creative sector tends to locate and outline the characteristics of these regions in order to derive conclusions on the location decision of agents in the creative sector. Fritsch and Stützer (2006) apply a variable for the share of bohemians indicating the variety of cultural amenities and an index for the provision of public goods measuring the employees in public health care and education. The authors also analyse if growth in employment has an impact on the regional distribution of the creative sector. The factor tolerance is captured by the share of foreign-born people analogous to Florida's "melting-pot-index" and can be interpreted as a variable for locational openness.

Empirical cross sectional analyse on German IAB[17] data for the year 2004 show that economic agents working in the creative sector cluster in tolerant and open places comprising the share of foreign born people. The results do, however, raise the question of whether the presence of foreign-born people really represents economic integration or just settlement in the same economic region.

---

16 The index for tolerance consists of a variable for the employment rate of non-western citizens, the ratio of foreign western and non-western citizens, a variable for the share of bohemians, a variable for cultural opportunities, the unemployment rate and an index for the provision of public goods. The tolerance indicator has to be interpreted as an overall indicator for the "quality of place", i.e. it is a measure of the locational condition.

17 Nuremberg Research Data Centre of the Federal Employment Agency (FDZ) at the Institute for Employment Research (IAB), Nuremberg, Germany.

Their results, however, follow other empirical findings on the interaction of innovation and diversity of agents in Germany (see, for instance, Niebuhr 2006).

Fritsch and Stützer analyse further if high shares of creative professionals can be explained by the provision of public goods; the index for public goods can be interpreted as a locational conditions. In the empirical analysis, Fritsch and Stützer conclude that the share of employees in the educational and health care sector is important, while labour market opportunities play a minor role in the agent's choice of location.

Applying the creative sector as explanatory variables in multivariate analyses and controlling for the former GDR, Fritsch and Stützer (2006) find a positive and highly significant correlation between the creative sector, location, and regional growth. However, they further show that the size of the regional labour market is not as strongly linked to the location of the creative sector as the size of cultural amenities (bohemians).

The author's results suggest that the creative sector especially concentrates in cities such as Stuttgart, Munich and Frankfurt, i.e. the share of creative professionals in rural areas is generally smaller. The results from Fritsch and Stützer (2006) also show that some smaller German cities such as Erlangen and Coburg are listed on the overall "creative sector index" at the top of all 439 districts. Fritsch and Stützer, however, apply a simple linear OLS regression. The strengths of the relation between the independent and dependent variables is measured and captured with beta coefficients. The authors' conclude that the direction of causality is unexplained by the econometric model used. The paper suffers from a methodological point of view since no theoretical model is supplied by the authors.

Hansen (2007): The Swedish creative sector. The Swedish contribution aims to answer the research questions of where the creative sector is located, what determines that location, and what the interaction between the creative sector and economic growth is. The empirical research includes 81 Swedish labour market regions. Hansen (2007) investigates, besides indicators for technology (interpreted as the business climate) and talent (share of persons with a bachelor degree or above), indicators for tolerance which affect locational conditions and are said to attract the creative sector. Technology is captured by the variables of firm start-ups and a variable measuring the production in high-tech industries as a regional aggregation relative to the national one (called tech-pole index).

Investigating the average educational level for the creative sector, Hansen shows that the level of education is higher for agents working in the creative sector (approximately 40 percent hold a graduate degree). Furthermore, the relationship between agents with a graduate degree and occupied in the creative sector is 94 percent. Because of lacking historical data. Hansen uses the talent variable (share of persons with a graduate degree) as a proxy for the creative sector to look at population and employment growth.

The indicator tolerance is composed by a variable measuring the share of cultural agents in a region (bohemians). Another indicator accounts for the share of people from non-western countries in the local labour markets ("integration index"), and two further variables convey the economic and social openness which quantify the percentage of foreign-born people from non-western countries ("openness 1") and the percentage of all foreign-born people in the population ("openness 2"). Applying several econometric analyses, Hansen (2007) presents the results that the variables "openness 1" and bohemians have a significant impact on the location of people with a graduate degree. According to the results the largest effect comes from the bohemians. In a static analyses, Hansen finds a correlation between the creative sector and the variables bohemians, "openness 1", and "openness 2".

Hansen (2007) presents further that the link between the variables for technology (business climate) and regional growth is unknown, but the results for the creative sector on regional growth is positively significant. Analysing the three factors talent, tolerance, and technology on population as well as employment growth, it is concluded that technology is less important than the regional locational factor tolerance (bohemians and openness 1), and the talent variable, or the share of people with a graduate degree.

Overall, his results are that the labour market regions of the three biggest cities Stockholm, Gothenburg and Malmö appear to be the most competitive regions in terms of the location of the creative sector, talent and tolerance, but also with respect to technology. The university city Uppsala, nearby Stockholm, also appears successful in this context.[18]

Kröhnert et al. (2007): Ranking of Germany's Federal States. Kröhnert et al. (2007) contribute to the technology, talent and tolerance debate with an investigation of the 16 Federal States of Germany (German Laender). Their research simply rank the Federal States on the "creativity index" like Florida (2002). They also measure the growth of the indicators between 2000 and 2005 among the Laender regarding technology, talent and tolerance.

In their first step, they develop indices for talent and technology analogous to Florida. The talent index is measured by using micro-census data, whereas technology is captured by the variables of expenditure on research and development, patents per capita, and

---

18 In a similar study by Mellander and Florida (2007), the authors reach the same conclusion. The difference between that study and the one mentioned above is, that Mellander and Florida also investigated the linkages to universities and its impact on regional economic growth.

high-tech patents per capita. A significant relation between a high share of patents per capita and the creative sector is given.

The tolerance index diverges in its design. Besides measuring ratios of foreigners in the population and labour market, they integrate two more qualitative indices in order to measure the tolerance and acceptance of ethnic-cultural diversity in the home population. The first indicator is the share of local votes for right wing parties for the Bundestag election in 2005. The second one is the ratio of acceptance in response to xenophobic statements. Both indicators can be interpreted as the acceptance of foreign-born residents by the localised population. Kröhnert et al.'s (2007) results suggest that "intolerant" German Laender have a relatively lower share of people in the creative sector.

Further, they show that the city states of Berlin and Hamburg score especially high in the case of the location of the creative sector. Kröhnert et al. (2007) investigate German Laender, therefore this result is not a surprise, since there is a missing link to the regional and city level. Further, the causal effect - i.e. if a *ceteris paribus* change of the share of the creative sector effects, for instance, the share of patent per capita or *vice versa* - is uncertain.

Möller and Tubadji (2009): New empirical evidence for Germany. Möller and Tubadji (2009) investigate two basic hypotheses of Florida's (2002) *The rise of the creative class*. Hypothesis one is that the regional concentration of the creative sector will contribute to employment or wage growth. Hypothesis two is that the creative sector will be attracted by a higher regional concentration of bohemians. Using IAB-individual data (IABREG) for West-Germany between 1975 and 2004, they run a dynamic panel regression with fixed effects to test both hypotheses. Möller and Tubadji's (2009) paper is interesting because of a few different aspects.

First, they use a similar definition to that of Florida. For that reason, they divide the creative sector into bohemians, "(super) creative core" and "creative professionals". Diverging in design, the bohemian-definition comes from Boschma and Fritsch (2007).[19] More interesting, as an alternative to Florida's (2002) concept, Möller and Tubadji (2009) introduce three further variables: the share of high-skilled employment, the share of employment in mathematics, engineering, the natural sciences and technical work (MENT), as well as the share of the employment in the humanities.

---

19 Boschma and Fritsch (2007) use Florida's (2002) concept of the creative sector and try to find comparable results for 450 European regions in eight different countries by using the ISCO 88 definition. Boschma and Fritsch (2007) run different regressions with various specifications. Their results show that the location of bohemians affect the regional pooling of employment in the creative sector.

Second. the paper is strong from a methodological point of view. Most of the literature on the creative sector interprets the correlation in a (cross-section) regression or bivariate analysis as causal linkages. however. a reverse causality is also plausible. Furthermore. the analyses presented in the economic literature on the creative sector faces mostly problems with endogeneity. Since Möller and Tubadji (2009) apply a dynamic panel estimation (GMM). they are able to reduce the problems with endogeneity. They include lag-variables and regional fixed effects (FE). With regional FE it is possible to control for omitted variables and for unobserved heterogeneity.

Their results show that the concentration of the creative sector contributes to employment and wage growth. Their hypothesis was that a concentration of bohemians results in a concentration of creative agents. Their findings for 323 German districts. however. show no supportive results for this hypothesis. This is in contrast to Shaprio (2006) or Boschma and Fritsch (2007) and Falck et al. (2009). Möller and Tubadji do find results that support their assumption that the employees of the creative sector prefer to live in strong economic regions. The clustering of high-skilled employment in one region does as well force regional employment and economic growth.

However. besides their strong and clear documentation. Möller's and Tubadji's (2009) weak point is that their empirical work is not based on a theoretical model. Furthermore. the important assumption by Florida. which is the self-reinforcing of already localised creative professionals. is also not investigated by Möller and Tubadji.

Table A.1.2 in the appendix summarises the above studies in alphabetical order and briefly shows the relation between the creative sector and its effect on city and regional growth.

2.3. General criticism on the central theories and the literature

The reviewed studies operationalise the creative sector in the analysis of urban development. One result is that corresponding concepts and their interpretations are limited. since most studies simply map the distribution of the creative sector and apply some simple correlation models. However. the economic situation is more complex. There has been some criticism in the literature of the concept and the methodology used in these studies. for instance from Asheim and Hansen (2008). Glaeser (2005). Hansen (2007). Peck (2005). or Storper and Scott (2009). This criticism is important. and is thus briefly discussed in following.

First, recall from section 2.1 that Florida (2002) captures human capital in a different way than by just conceptualising it as educational attainment. Given the definition of the creative sector, which is very close to a qualification-based definition, this measure is strongly correlated with the measure of educational attainment (Glaeser 2005; Hansen 2007). Glaeser's (2005) main critique is that Florida (2002) argues that the effects of "creative (human) capital" are stronger than the effects coming from "educational (human) capital". Using data for 242 regions in the United States in 1990, Glaeser (2005) does some simple OLS regressions in his review of Florida's (2002) *The rise of the creative class*. Glaeser (2005) runs the regressions separately for population growth on the share of local workers in the "(super) creative core", patents per capita, Florida's gay index and the bohemian index. One conclusion is that there is some relatively strong indication that bohemians have relevance for population growth. More importantly, he shows that there is a lack of evidence that "creative (human) capital" is the key variable for urban population growth and not, in general, human capital. Glaeser (2005) therefore concludes that "creative (human) capital" is not exclusively relevant for growth, while "educational (human) capital" is.[20,21] Marrocu and Paci (2010) contribute to this discussion through an empirical investigation on creative agents with university degrees ("creative-graduates"), without university degrees ("non-creative-graduates"), and bohemians in 257 European regions. They find that the highly educated group of creative-graduates is the most relevant group for explaining the growth of total factor productivity. In addition to the debate on human capital, Glaeser (2005) further argues that there is less new crediting the value of economic agents. This in light of the fact that *inter alia* Adam Smith (2003), Alfred Marshall (1920a) or Becker (1975) - so the argument - contributed to the modern discussion of generating economic growth through human capital.

Second, the aspect that city's and region's economic successes comes from being attractive places is also highlighted by Glaeser (2005). Especially against the background of low transportation costs, few cities and regions have a comparative advantage in attracting economic agents, so the argument coming from Glaeser. Therefore, the idea of Florida's cultural amenity of places (bohemians, diversity or public provision) to attract economic agents is not new in the discussion of urban economics and in its necessity for urban policy

---

20 Florida et al. (2008) reacted to this critique with an empirical paper on 331 metropolitan statistical areas in the US in year 2000. They find out that human capital (educational measure) and the creative sector (occupational measure) affect regional growth in different ways. Human capital outperforms in affecting regional income. The creative sector performs better in accounting for regional labour productivity. Florida et al. (2008) use structural equation models and path analysis to obtain these results.

21 On the contrary, Hansen (2008) presents a correlation between the share of human capital (agents with a bachelor degree or above) and the share of the creative professionals, with an R^2 of 94 percent for Sweden. However, in the Swedish context, only 40 percent of the creative professionals hold a graduate degree, which shows how substantially different the two concepts are in the Swedish context.

(Glaeser 2005). Another point in the discussion is that the creative sector depends heavily on the socio-economic development status (Asheim and Hansen 2008). Since urban and regional development depends on an evolutionary process that is path dependent (see also Storper and Scott 2009), the creative sector and its policy instruments are not part of a "one-size-fits-all" approach. The economic potential through the creative sector has to be contextualised to the particular underlying economic system.[22] For example, agents in Europe are generally considered to be less mobile than economic agents in the United States (Hansen 2007; Suedekum 2010). In Europe the role of the public sector is also much more important than in the US; furthermore, in US cities fewer city centres exist, the consequence of which is that US cities have to deal more with the (re-)creation of urban (locational) conditions than European cities. Following that argument, the competition for economic agents between cities and regions is a different size in the United States than in Europe. On the other hand, through demographic changes towards an aging society European cities also have to compete for human capital. However, studies for European cities have to take this different context into account.

A fourth main critique addresses the definition of the creative sector and how to operationalise this definition, the argument being that the definition appears to be a quasi-arbitrary decision. For example, cabinetmakers are not considered in the definition of the creative sector, since furniture is considered as a low-tech and less-knowledge intensive product. The question is, however, are architects more creative than cabinetmakers? To provide an answer to the question is to link to a study about traditional industries by Maskell and Lorenzen (2004b). They investigate the question of how innovative low-tech industries are on the basis of the furniture industry.[23] Maskell and Lorenzen (2004b) raise attention to the innovative ability of cabinetmakers, since, for instance, the inventor and founder of *Leg Godt* (LEGO) was a cabinet maker. In the Danish context, cabinet making and, especially, furniture design are considered to be innovative and creative. Both together are one of Denmark's biggest export products.[24] This example, however, shows that the discussion about what creativity could be is one of the most controversial aspects of this discussions (for a further discussion, see, for instance, Storper and Scott 2009).[25]

---

22 For the discussion on the varieties of economic systems, i.e. varieties-of-capitalism, see, for example, Elsner and Hanappi (2008) as well as Hall and Soskice (2004).

23 Porter disagrees that there is "'such a thing as a low-tech industry" (Porter 1998, 86). He argues that there are many low-tech companies which are companies who fail to be innovative and to use new technologies or to adopt new innovations.

24 The UK definition for the creative sector - the so called creative industries - therefore considers handcrafts as creative professions as well.

25 Asheim and Hansen (2008) suggest that the creative sector can be broken down into further groups which have different knowledge bases - namely an analytical, a synthetic, and a symbolic knowledge base. An analytical knowledge base is ideally characterised by solving research problems and generating new knowledge. Examples of economic agents working in analytical knowledge based professions are

Fifth, as presented, Florida (2002) measures the openness (tolerance) of regions. For the analysis he also uses a kind of ethnic-cultural diversity measure (i.e. diversity of economic agents by nationality). However, some authors recognise in the discussion that the ethnic-cultural diversity might hinder the knowledge exchange between different ethnic and cultural groups and cause adverse productivity effects. A multitude of languages raises communication and network costs due to cultural distance (Alesina and Ferrara 2005) such as debilitation of trust (Maskell et al. 1998). Ottaviano and Peri (2006) stress that a core of shared norms might be necessary to realise the potential benefits of the diversity of economic agents. In the context of the creative sector, these possibly negative effects, such as the possible lack of collective institutions and co-ordination mechanisms, are not discussed in the literature.[26] The last general criticism point out in the context of diversity that economically successful cities are places where individual agents (and agents working in the field of the creative professionals) are concentrated. As a result, cities pull migrants (internal and external) and move in for economic participation and rent seeking. This driving force is simply rational. But, in the literature about the creative sector high levels of ethnic-cultural agents (tolerance) are associated with economic and employment growth. Moreover, these diverse agents are linked to culture in the city. This economically rational choice has less to do with how tolerant a city is. It has and more to do with how attractive a city is from an economic perspective (for a further discussion, see, *inter alia*, Peck 2005; Sassen 2001). i.e. the economic approach to regions and cities starts with decision making agents.

2.4. Interim summary and conclusions

Summary. Florida (2002) was influenced by the economics of human capital. He operationalised the concept of human capital for the concept of the creative cities. i.e. cities economically driven by the creative sector, which is defined as an emerging cohort of

---

physicists, mathematicians and university professionals. As an ideal type, a synthetic knowledge base refers to solving practical problems, for e.g. architects and engineering related professionals. Writers and artists professionals are ideally working within the symbolic knowledge base. The characterisation of this knowledge base deals with cultural meaning. This approach brings up a more structured view to the problem of conceptualising the creative sector. The authors conclude that it reduces the complexity of understanding knowledge creation and innovation processes (Hansen et al. 2005; Asheim and Hansen 2008).

26 The literature on the creative sector neglect that innovation, production and the exchange of (collective) goods have a social character. Thereby, forms of trust give stable expectations (contingent trust) for future actions among economic agents (for the further discussion on trust, see, *inter alia*, Elsner 2004, 2005). Trust enhances the effectiveness of coordination and reduces transaction costs and complexity, that is the overall social interaction of production and innovation between economic agents (see, for instance, Elsner 2004, 2005; Maskell and Lorenzen 2004a). A form of collective institution of coordination mechanisms are clusters and networks.

economic agents working in the fields of engineering, health, science and others. Jacobs' (1969) concept of urban neighbourhoods and the diversity of economic agents was recognised by Florida (2002). According to Florida (2002; 2003; 2004; 2005), the diversity of economic agents contributes to creative cities' economic growth and competitiveness by positively impacting knowledge and human capital. Albeit, the creative city concept is hard to operationalise and a theoretical model is missing (see also Glaeser 2005; Peck 2005), the creative sector has an increasing influence on research studying urban and regional economics.

To sum up, within the literature it is frequently argued that the creative sector plays a major role in economic growth (wages and employment) of cities and regions. The creative sector is further supposed to be a factor for innovative processes and to firm new businesses. Regarding the aspect of the diversity of economic agents, the overall arguments in the reviewed literature are that it brings varieties of knowledge bases, experiences and (knowledge) networks. It is argued that diversity raises the varieties of entrepreneurial activities, meaning the transformation of ideas and inventions into novel businesses. Further, diversity is interpreted as a locational condition by most economic literature. Finally, to the best of my knowledge there is no paper focusing on Florida's hypothesis of the self-reinforcing process of creative professionals.

Conclusions. The above section documented the main critiques of the literature on the creative sector. Despite these critiques, the creative sector is special due to the fact that it focuses on professions, and this differentiates it primarily from the classifications of education, qualification or industry applied in most economic work (for more discussion, see, for example, Glaeser 2005; Möller and Tubadji 2009). A more differentiated approach to the common human capital definition is appropriate, since human capital refers to productive and creative abilities, skills or experiences. Therefore, due to this definition, it contributes to the scientific discussion.

In the following, I contribute to the discussion with a model, which considers agents as creative or non-creative. This is an important response to the criticism addressing the definition of the creative sector. The available theories and results on the creative sector cannot satisfactorily explain their importance to economic and employment growth. I put forward a theoretical framework, which helps to explain why the creative sector is important for employment growth. The model further contributes to the discussion of the self-reinforcing process of the creative sector. The applied model is mainly based on a human capital model coming from Suedekum (2006, 2008). At this point, the economic thinking starts with the assumptions and not with collecting and analysing of data.

3. Theoretical framework

The studies presented thus far on the creative sector generally do not apply any theoretical model. Rather, the most studies show more descriptively the relative importance of the creative sector for the economy. Therefore, it is the aim of this chapter to introduce theoretical arguments and a human capital based model that determines the regional dynamics of location and growth within an economy, with regard to the creative economy.

This chapter is organised as follows. section 3.1 provides arguments which support the underlying idea that some agents are considered to be more creative than others. The arguments address a critical point in the discussion on creativity: Florida selects agents apparently by chance, including those he supposes to be creative, whereas others are not considered at all.[1] Using the categorisation from Murphy et al. (1991) for the allocation of talent, this work argues that agents select their profession by ability. Building on this result, I define creativity to specific abilities and select hereafter the creative professions. This classification is realised for empirical analysis in chapter 4. Section 3.2 contributes to the discussion of the creative sector with a modified human capital model by Suedekum (2006, 2008). The model helps to explain why the creative sector is important to overall employment growth. It further explains why cities and regions with high numbers of creative agents grow faster than others. It delivers the arguments answering the first three research questions outlined in the first chapter.[2] Finally, in section 3.3 a summary with conclusions provides a framework for this thesis' content and its empirical research.

3.1. The creative professionals, or why some agents are considered to be creative and others not

In the discussion on creative professionals, Florida (2002) argues that this group is important to economic growth. In the following, I introduce arguments coming from Murphy

---

1 Cf. for this discussion section 2.3, on the general criticism.
2 Recall from chapter 1, that research question 1 is "How important is the creative sector for employment growth?", research question 2 is "How relevant are the economic effects originating from diversity?", and research question 3 is "Is there a self-reinforcing process of the pooled creative professionals?".

et al. (1991) that help to deliver answers to the important question of why some agents are considered to be creative, whereas others are not. Although Florida is guided by concepts of human capital models, the latter question is of particular importance because Florida's classification of creative professionals is not based in a systematic classification but rather seems to follow a random decision.

Murphy et al. (1991) introduce a one-sector model to explain how economic agents become entrepreneurs, i.e. an economic agent willing and able to transform ideas (invention) into a marketed product (innovation). The authors present a two-sector model, explaining that the ablest agent always shifts into the sector with the highest possible rents. In the model, they introduce rent seeking into the one-sector model to explain why some economic agents become rent seekers and not creative (or productive) entrepreneurs (or employees).

Murphy et al. also empirically analyse the ability distribution of individual agents and their effect on economic growth. The authors build a model with two types of individuals. They can either work in a rent creating or in a rent seeking sector. The model shows that the distribution of the two types of individuals depends on returns to ability. Building on empirical evidence from Barrow (1991), the authors suggest that the size of the rent seeking sector might be determined by government consumption. Alternatively, an occupational based approach is suggested. The authors provide evidence for rent creating and rent seeking in a one-sector model based on the latter approach. Murphy et al. use two professional groups to test their hypothesis: engineers and lawyers. It is assumed that engineers rather than lawyers improve technology, create new products, and raise the rate of economic growth. Lawyers seem to distribute income and wealth. The empirical results further suggest that the latter professional group reduce the rate of economic growth. Lawyers are much more engaged in the distribution of income than its creation.

In the following, I build my argumentation for the classification of creative professionals on this model. In doing so, it is assumed that production technologies are imitated, and every agent's productivity is therefore equal. Agents have different abilities, however, and therefore are different with respect to the operation of the technology. Hence, profits differ due to agent's different abilities. More able agents earn more than less able agents. The increase in profits is due to the fact that the output increases with the ability, and therefore creative agents can use their advantage in ability to increase their firm's size and growth. However, the costs for production do not rise. As a result, there are increasing returns on ability. When the most able agent become creative, he organises production in the most efficient way. In the case of constant returns to scale, the most able agent will dominate and capture the whole market. In the case of diminishing returns, the most able agent's ability to increase the firm's size is limited. Moreover, growth is specified by the evolution of the technology. The state of technology is determined by the most able agent's ability in the previous period. As a consequence, the maximum growth rate is determined by the ability of the most creative agents.

Expanding on this, it is possible to discuss the distribution of creative agents in a two sector model. Each sector has its own production function. In all other respects, the sectors are identical. the preferences are of Cobb-Douglas-type. Therefore. the same income is spent on a sector good for each period. A sector's productivity is determined by the ability of the ablest agent in the sector. In a social optimum, the most able agent is allocated to sector one and the second most able agent to sector two. As a result. growth rates differ between the two sectors, but both sectors grow with the maximum growth rate. But. in equilibrium each agent seeks (quasi) rents and these rents are higher in the first sector. therefore also the second most able agent switches to the first sector. As a result, the second sector grows at a lower rate, since the first sector absorbs the most able agents. In the context of the creative sector, an example of a second most able agents becoming creative is that of a professional organist. If the market for the organist is small in size and no high profits are paid, he becomes the second best pianist. In this case, people are willing to pay more to listen to his piano playing than to his organ music. Another reason for distorted distributions among economic agents between sectors are transaction costs or (labour) market barriers. Economic agents prefer sectors where it is easier to start firms. and sector's that are regarded as less capital intensive. Sectors with less capital intensity are more attractive for starting up new businesses and firms. since product or business introduction are already combined with high costs (see. for example. Murphy et al. 1991). In particular. agents prefer new sectors such as the creative sector is. Moreover. if we assume a model with two cities (or regions) and free mobility between the two cities. the most able agents would be strongly attracted to the more open city in order to increase income.

Rent seeking also plays a role in this argument. Agents with a sufficiently high ability can either become creative. or work as rent seekers. An individual agent can choose to become. for instance. an entrepreneur or lawyer. an engineer or technical officer. a musician or pastor. and. a manager or a military staff officer. His descision depends on his ability. but also on the conditions of business such as market size or contract certainty. For example. under a regime of weak copyrights for music there is possibly less motivation for the most able musician to produce music. The weak protection regime reduces (possibly future) profits and. moreover. the motivation for the production of music. This helps to explain why a sector attracts a different type of agent into it than other sectors. This example shows further that ability is often generally distributed, rather than specifically distributed according to occupation. The distribution of agents sometimes relies on (institutional) norms.[3] Higher transaction costs and larger rent seeking institutions reduce creative activities and expand the rent seeking sector: One result is that the greater the rent seeking sector, the lower the rate of growth, since the ablest agents are absorbed. In some countries, for instance, armies are able to pay the highest wages. As a result, these countries absorb not only stocks of physical and financial capital, but also human capital. However, since rent seeking depends mainly on the institutional settings within countries, Murphy et al.'s model has not been selected to explain the impact of the creative sector on economic growth. The model rather points to institutional differences across countries, and not across regions within a country. Nevertheless, the model supports the argument that the creative sector has to be contextualised in light of the particular underlying economic system, since countries with large public institutions may absorb (creative) economic agents. More importantly, with the presented arguments and neglecting institutional settings, it is possible to demonstrate why some economic agents choose professions depending on abilities, and why some professions can be considered as more creative than others. As a result, Murphy et al.'s model supports the creative sector argument; with an occupational based approach it is possible to classify the agents by creative ability. This classification of occupations by ability is made in chapter 4.

3.2. A simple model of the creative city

This section provides a theoretical model to show the importance of creative agents for employment growth. It allows for the derivation of first results, answers to the first, second and third research questions.

The model relies on a human capital model developed by Moretti (2004) and adjusted by Suedekum (2006, 2008). Suedekum developed this basic model to investigate whether high shares of initial human capital (high-skilled agents) increase high-skilled employment growth, and in doing so discusses the underlying relationship between human capital and overall employment growth. Suedekum further addresses the question of whether human capital spillovers (i.e. externalities) are associated with the educational level of agents. There are private and social returns of human capital, that is higher average wages as a result of higher average level of human capital. Consequently, human capital is assumed to have a social and public character (see, *inter alia,* Lucas 1988). In his investigation Moretti finds that the regional supply of college graduates raises the wage of less educated groups. He concludes therefore that the level of the average education has a social return.

---

3 In the Murphy et al. model, it is furher argued that rent seeking has no creative component at all. This assumption is very different from Florida's definition. Recall that his definition also includes professionals, for instance, in legal services which are in fact rent seeking professions.

Table 3.1.: Modelling the creative city

List of variables

p_Y = price of the good, set to 1
Y = tradable good
$N = (N_c + N_l)$ = composite of creative and less-creative agents
N_c = number of creative agents
N_l = number of less-creative agents
$S = N_c/N$ = Share of creative agents
A = productivity parameter
ϕ = local amenities (idiosyncratic city effect)
γ = strength of human capital externality, $\gamma \geq 0$
j, i = city
w^{N_c} = wage of creative agents
w^{N_l} = wage of less creative agents
S^* = steady state

Suedekum (2006, 2008) use the model to explore whether regions with low numbers of high-skilled agents converge to regions with high numbers of high-skilled agents. That is, regions with low shares of high-skilled agents tend to grow faster than regions with high shares of high-skilled agents. The former tend to catch up (for more discussion, see, for example, Barrow 1991). The paper also delivers empirical evidence for his model. As a result, the author finds that cities with high levels of skilled agents initially grow faster in employment than unskilled cities. More importantly, cities with an initially high share of high-skilled agents face lower growth rates in such high-skilled employment afterwards. Hence, he does not observe a self-reinforcing spatial concentration, findings no converging tendency between regions. Suedekum's (2006; 2008) observation and results indicate that total employment increases since low-skilled employment grows faster than the high-skilled employment (growth rate) declines.

In the following, I present a model of the creative city. In my model, I assume that higher shares of creative professionals raise the employment growth rate of their group, and overall employment growth. Furthermore, creative professionals are attracted by local amenities. The model mainly builds on Suedekum (2006; 2008). Table 3.1 presents a list of variables used in the model.

In each city j firms produce a homogeneous good Y_j with the help of creative and less-creative labour. The number of creative agents is N_c and the number of less-creative agents is N_l. Suppose that there is a Cobb-Douglas technology that employs creative and less-creative agents, where productivity is determined by a parameter A_j.

Then the production function is given by:

$$Y_j = A_j N_{l,j}{}^\alpha N_{c,j}{}^{1-\alpha} \quad 0 < a < 1. \tag{3.1}$$

Y_j is traded on the market without trading costs, meaning the price of the product p_Y is the same everywhere and set to 1. Both input factors, creative and less-creative agents, are paid to their marginal product. The logarithm of wages (to base e) for less-creative and creative agents are, respectively:

$$log(w_j^{N_l}) = log(\alpha) + log(A_j) + (1 - \alpha)log\left(\frac{S_j}{1 - S_j}\right) \tag{3.2}$$

and

$$log(w_j^{N_c}) = log(1 - \alpha) + log(A_j) - \alpha log\left(\frac{S_j}{1 - S_j}\right) \quad . \tag{3.3}$$

$S_j = N_{c,j}/N_j < 1$ is the share of creative professionals in city j, whereas N_j is the composite of creative and less-creative agents ($N_{c,j} + N_{l,j}$). An increase in the number of creative agents raises the wage of the less-creative agents (while the wages of creative agents decrease), as we can see, spillover further raises the overall productivity. There is a further assumption in the productivity parameter A_j, which depends endogenously on the share of creative professionals S_j. I assume, in particular, a factor of human capital externality and of local amenities:

$$log(A_j) = log(\phi_j) + \gamma \cdot log(1 + S_j) \quad . \tag{3.4}$$

The potential strength of the human capital externality is given by $\gamma > 0$ and local amenities of city j are captured by an idiosyncratic city effect ϕ_j. The characteristics of local amenities may be linked to the share of creative agents as the former affect the location. Creative agents are assumed to value and choose those places with high local amenity characteristics.[4] Suedekum (2006, 2008), Moretti (2004), and Rauch (1993) stressed in their models that those city characteristics are (relatively) time-invariant. This is especially true for the geographical conditions of a location such as weather or access to the sea.[5]

---

4 The assumption that high-skilled agents are more mobile than less-skilled agents is consistent with empirical evidence, see, for example, Hunt (2006).

5 Rauch (1993), for instance, controls for coastal locations in his empirical work. He assumes that coastal locations have a recreational amenity effect on human capital. Further the author argues that wages and rents are higher in port cities, since those cities gain from international trade. Moretti (2004) controls for unobserved characteristics across cities by using city specific fixed effects.

To keep things simple, I do not consider other relevant factors concerning location, such as agent's housing consumption, as Moretti (2004) or Rauch (1993) do.[6]

Consider what happens to the wages, if the number of creative agents increase in city j. Substituting equation 3.4 in 3.2 and 3.3, produces new equations that may be written as:

$$\frac{\partial log\left(w_j^{N_l}\right)}{\partial S_j} = \frac{1-\alpha}{S_j(1-S_j)} + \frac{\gamma}{1+S_j} \tag{3.5}$$

and

$$\frac{\partial log\left(w_j^{N_c}\right)}{\partial S_j} = -\frac{\alpha}{S_j(1-S_j)} + \frac{\gamma}{1+S_j} \ . \tag{3.6}$$

In the absence of human capital externalities ($\gamma = 0$) the wage of less-creative agents in city j ($w_j^{N_l}$) depends on the share of creative agents S_j. The wage of less-creative agents will be positively affected by an increase in creative agents. It is assumed that both agent groups are imperfect substitutes. The second term of equation 3.5 points to this argument: This wage effect will be even higher, i.e. reinforced, in the presence of human capital externalities $\gamma > 0$. The impact of an increase in the supply of creative agents S_j depends on the effect of γ, which is presented in equation 3.6. The important feature of equation (3.5) and (3.6) is that less-creative agents benefit from the increase in creative agents, and they benefit also in the absence of spillovers $\gamma = 0$. The wage of creative agents benefits only from the presence of spillovers $\gamma > 0$, otherwise the wage effect of $\gamma = 0$ is negative.

Given that I am interested in employment growth, it seems plausible to assume that there is a long-run relationship between the variables wage and employment growth, in other words the rate of wage growth should increase with employment growth. There should be a greater increase in the number of creative agents in cities with a high return on human capital. Whether agents are attracted to places with a high initial share of

6 I have also dropped out city specific (consumption) amenities. These amenities could depend endogenously on the local number of creative agents. The amenities could include cultural characteristic such as the diversity of economic agents or the share of bohemians. In the economic literature on creative agents, both are regarded as a factor for the attraction of creative professionals. Building on Suedekum's model (2006; 2008), it may be assumed that in the long run the value of city specific amenities are determined by the number of bohemians B and the diversity of economic agents δ , i.e. $log(\phi_j) = log(B_j) + \theta \cdot log(1 + \delta_j)$, where $\theta > 0$ is the potentially strength of social trust θ. An important feature of trust θ could be that the diverse composition of agents may determine the size of transaction costs resulting from cultural differences between (significant different) individual agents. Trust enhances the effectiveness of co-ordination and reduces transaction costs and complexity, that is the overall social interaction of production and innovation between economic agents (for further discussion on trust, see, for example, Elsner 2004, 2005; Maskell and Lorenzen 2004a). The number of bohemians is maybe relevant, since they are regarded to influence the location of the economic agents.

creative agents depends on the presence of the strengths of human capital externalities $\gamma > 0$. Otherwise, creative agents are attracted to cities with an initially low share of creative agents, meaning locations with an absence of spillover $\gamma = 0$. To illustrate this, assume for example that there are two cities i and j. Equation 3.7 demonstrates the model for the two cities i and j:

$$
\begin{aligned}
log(w_i^{N_c}) - log(w_j^{N_c}) &= \gamma log\left((1 + S_i) - log(1 + S_j)\right) \\
-\alpha &\left(log\left(\frac{S_i}{1-S_i}\right) - log\left(\frac{S_j}{1-S_j}\right)\right) + (log(\phi_i) - log(\phi_j)) \quad .
\end{aligned}
\tag{3.7}
$$

The agents are perfectly mobile, they can easily move from city i to j. Thus, price equalisation results due to less migration, and in the long run the nominal wages must be equalised across both cities i and j. The long run equilibrium of the nominal wage is obtained by $log(w_i^{N_c}) - log(w_j^{N_c}) = 0$, or:

$$
(1 + S_i)^{\gamma} \cdot \left(\frac{1}{S_i} - 1\right)^{\alpha} \cdot \phi_i = (1 + S_j)^{\gamma} \cdot \left(\frac{1}{S_j} - 1\right)^{\alpha} \cdot \phi_j \quad (\forall i, j).
\tag{3.8}
$$

Abstracting from exogenous local amenity distributions between the two cities $\phi_i = \phi_j$, equation 3.8 is in the long run in equilibrium where $S_i = S_j = S^*$ for all cities $\forall i, j$. In the absence of spillovers $\gamma = 0$, this equilibrium of S^* is stable, i.e. the cities' shares of creative agents should converge in the long run. This equilibrium is not stable in the presence of human capital externalities $\gamma > 0$. To further simplify the example, it is assumed that city j is a small city, the agents shares are constant in other cities, as given by the steady state S^*. Substituting $S^* = S_j$ in equation 3.8 and assuming $\phi_i = \phi_j$, there must be an equilibrium for city j. This equilibrium is not stable if high human capital externalities $\gamma > 0$ exists.[7]

However, figure 3.1 shows the wage disparity $w_j^{N_c} - w^{N_c*}$, whereas w^{N_c} is the average wage, for different strength of externality γ and as a function of S_j. Panel a of figure 3.1 shows a stable equilibrium for $S^* = S_j$ with a low strength of γ or $\gamma = 0$. The share of creative agents will increase (decrease) if the initial share of creative agents was below (above) S^*. Panel b and c demonstrate unstable equilibria (S' in panel b) and stable (S'' in panel b and S' or S'' in panel c). In panel d the externalities are strong enough to increase

---

7 For the further discussion, on means of setting the relative supply of creative agents to be unequally distributed, is to assume that city j has higher levels of local amenities. The equilibrium is not stable if the distribution of amenities is $\phi_i \neq \phi_j$. Given the assumption that creative agents value the level of amenities while less-creative agents do not, the relative supply of creative agents in city j is higher than in city i if $\phi_i < \phi_j$. The influence of this distribution could rely on, for instance, the number of bohemians. In the absence of spillovers, a standard result is that an increase in creative agents increases the wage of less-creative agents. The less-creative agents are relatively more productive in city j. In the opposite case, the creative agents accept lower wages, since they value having more local amenities: The share of creative agents further increases.

the shares of creative agents in city j, and there is a self-reinforcing process of regionally pooled creative agents: The initially high share of creative agents is followed by a high growth rate in the same employment group.

Figure 3.1.: The equilibrium of creative agents share S_j

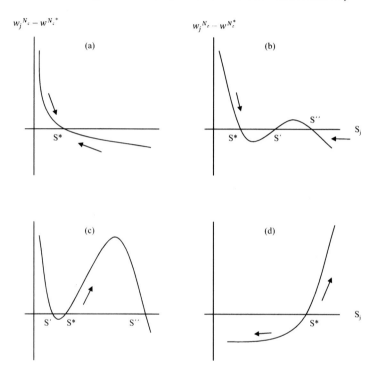

Notes: (a) $\gamma = 0$ or low γ; (b) intermediate γ; (c) high γ; (d) very high γ.
Source: Suedekum (2006). 8.

3.3. Interim summary and conclusions

Summary. Chapter 3 provides a theoretical approach to the fuzzy concept of the creative sector. I present two models built on Murphy et al. (1991) and Suedekum (2006).

Section 3.1 presents a model by Murphy et al. (1991) to support Florida's view that some agents contribute more to creativity, and thus to production, than others. The model presents the idea that the most able agent switches between both the rent creating and rent seeking sector. However, the model builds on Murphy et al.'s (1991) does not explain economic growth disparities within a country, but between countries.

More important, section 3.2 illustrates how the model built on Suedekum (2006) helps to explain whether the creative sector contributes to employment growth. The self-reinforcing process - i.e., that high shares of pooled creative agents lead to a higher growth rate within that specific employment group - is investigated. In the long run, if human capital externalities do not exist, $\gamma = 0$, the number of creative agents is constant and the model in equilibrium. In the opposite case, economic growth will positively depend on the initial share of creative agents if strong externalities exist, $\gamma > 0$. In cases where the rate of growth is negatively correlate with the initial share of creative agents, it might turn out that the externalities are not strong enough to increase further the shares of creative agents in regions with already high shares of pooled creative agents. However, this does not automatically mean that low externalities are negatively dependend on growth. Another explanation would be that there exists an imperfect substitution effect between creative and less-creative agents.

Conclusions. This theory will be confronted with empirical evidence in chapter 5. The empirical section of this work aims to investigate whether the evidence is consistent with Florida's (2002) theory of the self-reinforcing processes of regionally concentrated creative agents being due to strong externalities. The empirical analysis will, however, not quantify the size of potential externalities. If there is evidence for convergence, I may conclude that no strong spillovers occurs, in other words, that the neoclassical supply effect is strong enough to outbalance the inequalities between regions. In his contribution to the discussion, Moretti (2004) concludes that human capital externalities are a standard market failure, whereas the imperfect substitution effect between creative and less-creative agents is not.[8] The empirical work further investigates whether local amenities ϕ. i.e. here measured by the share of bohemians and the diversity of economic agents, have an overall influence on regional employment growth (and on the location of creative agents).

The theoretical approach brought together in this chapter is clearly different from other papers on the creative sector. However, before studying the problems encountered in the empirical work through estimations, it is first important to introduce the work's main and minor hypotheses and the research design (chapter 4). In following, a few more detailed concepts are introduced in the subsequent fifth chapter. Both chapters are content of part II, empirical analysis.

---

8 Policy implications should therefore depend on whether imperfect substitutions occur or market failure arises, and this is considered in the conclusions to the empirical analysis.

Part II.

Germany's creative sector and its impact on employment growth: Empirical analysis

4. Hypotheses and research design

Hypotheses are proposed explanations for empirical observations. Establishing hypotheses helps to determine what conclusions can be drawn from the empirical evidence. Naturally, caution has to be taken in the interpretation of data and its estimations. Keane (2010) argues that applied econometric models do not perfectly explain "true" correlations. The econometric models explain whether significant correlations exist, whereas economic theory and common sense help to specify the econometric models and to judge whether causalities exist (Keane 2010; Studenmund 2006). After all, the hypotheses determine how useful the results are for policy evaluation (Keane 2010), and "what we can learn about the real world from a sample" (Studenmund 2006, 112). In this chapter, the research questions presented in section 1.1 are narrowed down and refined into hypotheses. Furthermore, the decision rules for accepting or rejecting the hypotheses are presented. I further contribute to the question of how the empirical research was carried out, by explaining the research's design. Most important, the final definition of the creative sector used in the work is highlighted. Naturally, the chapter 4 closes with a summary.

4.1. Main hypotheses

To structure the empirical analysis, I start with the main hypotheses. The econometric work seeks to shed light on the creative sector (research question 1) and on diversity (research question 2). The creative sector and diversity are supposed to contribute to economic growth and, furthermore, both variables are assumed to capture the "creative capacity" of regions (Baycan-Levent 2010; Florida 2002; Gülümser et al. 2010; Wedemeier 2010b). An investigation is then presented into whether pooled creative agents have a self-reinforcing effect, as stated by Florida (2002) (research question 3).

Research question 1 and 2. Consider a simple model hypothesising that the total employment growth (Y_1) is a function of the share of the creative sector, which is divided into the share of creative professionals (X_1) and the share of bohemians (X_2). The creative sector is separated in this way, because it is assumed that bohemians are an economic and a locational factor. Against this background, I separate the creative sector into the two specific employment groups X_1 (share of creative professionals) and X_2 (share of bohemians).

Suppose further that the diversity of economic agents raises Y_1. Once again, diversity is divided into two sub-groups, creative professional diversity (X_3) and ethnic-cultural diversity (X_4). The simple model is then:

$$Y_1 = f(X_1, X_2, X_3, X_4) \ . \tag{4.1}$$

After reformulating the model, a typical linear regression equation used in modelling is:

$$Y_1 = \beta_0 + \beta_1 X_1 + \beta_2 X_2 + \beta_3 X_3 + \beta_4 X_4 + \epsilon_i \ . \tag{4.2}$$

In the above equation, β_1 and β_2 are expected to be positive, since it is assumed that the creative sector contributes positively to the rate of employment growth. The diversity of economic agents will be measured by an inverse Herfindahl-Hirschman Index, which is negative if the relative concentration is high and positive in the presence of diversity. There are conflicting hypotheses about the expected signs of these coefficients, since the results can also be interpreted as indicating that clustering matters and not diversity. I will reject the null hypothesis if the values are positively or negatively significant.

Given the conflicting hypotheses about the expected signs, I apply a two-sided t-test (or two-tailed test) in which the null hypothesis states that the coefficients are equal to zero. Following from equation 4.2, the null and alternative hypothesis for all betas is $H_0 : \beta_k = 0$ and $H_A : \beta_k \neq 0$. The null hypothesis is rejected if the calculated t-value, t_k, is greater than the critical t-value t_c. The level of significance chosen for the two-tailed test is 10 percent. A disadvantage of a two-sided test is, however, that the possibility of a Type-I-Error - i.e. the rejection of a "true" null hypothesis - is twice as high for a two-sided than for a one-sided test (see, for example, Studemund 2006).[1]

Research question 3. Whether pooled creative professionals have a self-reinforcing process, meaning the contribution from the initial size of the creative professional's group to employment growth among the creative professionals, is the question posed by research question 3. Consider a simple model in which the growth rate among the creative professionals (Y_2) is a function of the share of the creative professionals (X_5) and the share of

---

1 The amount of 10 percent has to be distributed between two rejection regions (two critical t-values) (Studemund 2006).

bohemians (X_6). Suppose the hypothesising model is:

$$Y_2 = f(X_5, X_6) \ . \tag{4.3}$$

then the corresponding regression equation could be:

$$Y_2 = \beta_0 + \beta_5 X_5 + \beta_6 X_6 + \epsilon_i \ . \tag{4.4}$$

Following Florida's assumptions. I expect that a high initial share of creative professionals raises the growth rate of the number of creative professionals. Once again. bohemians are assumed to affect the location of the creative professionals. Bohemians are therefore not considered in Y_2. The null and alternative hypothesis for all betas is $H_0 : \beta_k = 0$ and $H_A : \beta_k \neq 0$. In testing the hypotheses. the level of significance is 10 percent. The hypotheses will be rejected if the estimated coefficients are significantly different from zero. If negative coefficients are obtained the results will also be considered since they might be useful for policy evaluation.

For all hypotheses. when a calculated t-value t_k is larger than a critical t-value t_c. the null hypothesis is rejected (Studenmund 2006). In consequence. the decision rule for the rejection of a null hypothesis is: for β_k. Reject H_0 if $|t_k| > t_c$. Table 4.1 presents a variable list with its corresponding research questions.

Table 4.1.: List of variables and its expected outcome

Research Question	Hypothesis	Expected sign
(1)	$\beta_1 X_1 =$ Share of creative professionals on total employment growth Y_1	+
	$\beta_2 X_2 =$ Share of bohemians on total employment growth Y_1	+
(2)	$\beta_3 X_3 =$ Creative professionals diversity on total employment growth Y_1	+/-
	$\beta_4 X_4 =$ Ethnic-cultural diversity on total employment growth Y_1	+/-
(3)	$\beta_5 X_5 =$ Share of creative professionals on creative professionals growth Y_2	+/-
	$\beta_6 X_6 =$ Share of bohemians on creative professionals growth Y_2	+/-

4.2. Minor hypotheses

The fourth research question of this research is, "What does the regional distribution of creative professionals look like?" Some regions have more creative professionals than others. For example, the south of Germany is perceived as the most economically successful region in software development and automotive engineering. The agglomerated region of Cologne is known to be a media city, and Hamburg is regarded as being successful in publishing and the performing arts. Therefore, the creative sector is regarded as being highly concentrated in those locations within Germany. Thus the first minor hypothesis is that the creative sector is unequally distributed in Germany.

The fifth research question is, "Are cities places with a higher share of creative professionals?" This question is based on the assumptions of Florida (2002, 2003, 2005), but also others like Glaeser (1994, 2008). Those authors state that cities' ability to attract economic agents is higher than that of rural areas. This assumption is also connected to the first minor hypothesis. The second minor hypothesis, meanwhile, is that creative professionals are mainly concentrated in agglomerated regions.

4.3. Research design and the definition of the creative sector, creative class and high-skilled agents

Research design. The research for the empirical work presented here is organised as follows. Research questions 1 to 3 are analysed econometrically, and the results are presented in chapter 5 and discussed in chapter 6. The aim is to contribute to the theory, supplying new evidence on the creative sector in German regions and its impact on employment growth. Before I start with the econometric analysis, the data set is described and a descriptive statistical overview is provided. Furthermore, the specifications for the econometric models are presented in detail. This is relevant to narrowing down research questions 1 to 3 and the main hypotheses on the econometric analysis. Afterwards, the regression results are presented.

Research question 4 is also answered in the fifth chapter, which includes distribution tables and statistical maps. In general, the empirical results are generated for Germany on a regional level and are based on the IABS employment samples for the years 1977 to 2004. The data are arranged with STATA 9.2, and the maps are processed with Regio Graph 8.

The answers to research question 5 are provided in chapter 5 and 7. The fifth research question is analysed primarily with descriptive methods. Statistical material is delivered

Table 4.2.: Research questions and the research design

Research Questions	Hypotheses		Method	Chapter
	Main	Minor		
1. How important is the creative sector for employment growth?	1, 2	.	econometric model	3, 5, 6
2. How relevant are the economic effects originating from the diversity (of employment) on employment growth?	3, 4	.	econometric model	3, 5, 6
3. Is there a self-reinforcing process of pooled creative professionals?	5, 6	.	econometric model	3, 5, 6
4. What does the regional distribution of creative professionals look like?	.	1	descriptive statistics	5
5. (a) Are cities places of with a higher share of creative professionals.	.	2	descriptive statistics	5
and (b) what (urban) policy instruments strengthen creative sector employment?	.	.	descriptive	7

to supplement the answer provided. on whether higher shares of creative professionals can be found in cities.

Hereafter. policy instruments and strategies are discussed. I present policy findings for the city of Hamburg. This city, the second biggest city in Germany, is briefly presented with a focus on its economic transition to the service sector and upcoming creative sector. Afterwards, instruments and strategies to strengthen the city's creative sector are broadly discussed. This is the contribution to the second part of the fifth research question: "What (urban) policy instruments strengthen creative sector employment?". Such an extended method is valueable because it benefits from the statistical and empirical results and raises further questions. The novel results are useful for policy evaluation.

Table 4.2 shows the research plan for the empirical work. and how the different chapters contribute to the five research questions. Before studying the implications on employment growth. the following paragraph gives a clear cut definition of the creative sector.

The creative sector, creative class, and high-skilled agents. I apply two different definitions of the creative sector (**Definition 1 and 2**). In addition. I have included a skill-based definition to include an estimate of its effects (**Definition 3**). All three definitions contribute to the debate on measuring human capital.

In following. the creative sector is defined as a group of economic agents working in two sub-groups. one in the field of technology and one in the field of culture.[2] The

---

2 Since December 2009 an official working definition of the creative sector for Germany, the so-called

first group is composed of engineers, architects, and technicians; they are employed as technological agents.[3] The creative professionals working in the field of technology and engineering are supposed to have the ability to be creative and productively active, and as a result, they supposedly directly affect the rate of economic progress (cf. chapter 3 and Murphy et al. 1991). The assumption is that they have a greater ability for technological creativity, in other words, the more agents there are working as technological employees, *ceteris paribus*, the higher the employment growth rate. This highlights the importance of allocating economic agents to the productive activities of an economy.

Economic agents employed as bohemians - such as journalists, musicians, and actors - make up the second employment group within the creative sector. Bohemians are supposed to be a factor for the location of economic agents, but they are also assumed to generate economic income. Bohemians give an impulse to create and to request new products (product variety and product externality). Bohemians have a further role through signalling, or "in identifying creative milieus", and they present cultural creativity. The third point of the definition of creativity, so-called economic creativity, has not been considered, since the theoretical framework of chapter 3 does not capture agents' abilities to contribute to economic creativity. Furthermore, it is hard to find a clear cut definition of agents with economic creative ability. With this definition of agents working in the field of technology and in culture, I obtain a clear cut definition of a specific employment group, relating to Florida's (2002) creative class: the creative sector.[4]

The alternative to the first definition of the creative sector comes from Florida (2002).[5] This latter understanding also includes employed agents' economic creative abilities. The measure for agents with technological creative abilities differs slightly from the above approach to the creative sector, because it incorporates Florida's exact definition for classification of the creative class.[6]

"cultural and creative economy" (*Kultur- und Kreativwirtschaft*) definition, has been active after it was presented and accepted by the upper house of the German parliament (Bundesrat) (Söndermann 2009; Söndermann et al. 2009; Wirtschaftsministerkonferenz 2009). The definition of the German parliament is predominantly culturally oriented. Besides the cultural orientation of the German definition, it contains a few branches regarded as creative, for instance advertising, architecture or games-industry. This creative component of the official German working definition originates from the UK approach of "creative industries". An interesting review and discussion on the multiple methodologies and definitions of UK's "creative industries", Germany's "cultural (and creative) economy", Scandinavian's "experience economy" as well as others is given in a tech report commissioned by the European Commission (N.N. 2006). The main definition used in the present work is, however, technologically as well as culturally oriented.

3 The group is also known as MENT, mathematics, engineering, natural sciences and technical related work, see also Möller and Tubadji (2009).

4 In the appendix, table A.1.3 gives a detailed overview to the IAB-occupational classification of the creative sector.

5 In the appendix, table A.1.4 provides an overview to the IAB-occupational classification.

6 IAB-label 73 (foreman, work master) belongs to the definition of Florida's (2002) agents with techno-

For the second definition. I have chosen to use the expression "creative class", and for the first definition I use the name "creative sector", in order to help differentiate between the two sector concepts.

Alternatively, the third definition is a skill-based definition, which differentiates between the shares of low-, medium- (skilled)-, and high-skilled agents.[7] However, in the empirical analysis, I focus on the employed high-skilled agents, since authors such as Glaeser (2005) consider this group to be highly relevant to regional growth. Another argument is that the low-skilled employment group is influenced by the current economic situation and, moreover, that the medium-skilled employment group is too broad a definition, so that both skill-specific employment groups cannot be applied in the econometric analysis.

To sum up, I use two different sector concepts for creative professionals, the creative sector and the creative class, and a skill-based concept in addition, all of which are summarised in the following three definitions:

1. The creative sector is defined by agents with the ability to implement technological and cultural creativity (**Definition 1**).

2. An alternative (control) is Florida's definition of the creative class, and states that agents contribute technological, cultural, and economic creativity (**Definition 2**).

3. The third definition (control) measures the share of high-skilled agents, meaning the share of employed agents with a university degree (**Definition 3**).

4.4. Interim summary

In this chapter, the hypotheses, the research strategy, and finally the definitions of the creative sector, creative class, and high-skilled agents have been presented.

The hypotheses are developed to help ask what conclusions can be drawn from the empirical evidence. Against the background of the fourth chapter, the hypothesis are accepted or rejected, relying on the results and levels of significance of the investigation. However, one needs to be cautious in the interpretation of the empirical estimations made in the following chapters. The econometric models explain whether significant correlations exists, whereas economic theory and common sense help to specify the econometric models and to judge causalities. Clearly, the presented hypotheses determine how useful the results are for policy evaluation.

---

logical creative ability. This is different from the first definition. Table A.1.4 provides an overview to the IAB-occupational classification of the creative class.
7 Table A.1.5 gives an overview on this definition.

Moreover, the creative sector, and two alternatives to the creative sector are presented. First, the creative sector is defined as consisting of agents with the ability to implement technological and cultural creativity (**Definition 1**). The second definition is fixed by Florida's creative class, focusing on agents with the ability to bring out technological, cultural, and economic creativity (**Definition 2**). The third definition measures the shares of high-skilled agents (**Definition 3**).

5. Evidence on the creative sector

This chapter presents the empirical part of the thesis. The results are presented in chapter 5. but are discussed in chapter 6. which treats the implications of the empirical evidence. The empirical research on the creative sector is based on and guided by the economic literature and the above-presented theory. The theory on the model of the creative sector and city influences the empirical specifications. *Vica versa*, the empirical results on the creative sector and city will also influence to some degree the theory. However, based on the empirical analysis not everything that helps to explain the rate of employment growth in the context of the creative sector is observable, but rather, the empirical results will help to understand the theory and deliver information on the underlying structures and mechanisms.

5.1. Data and variable definitions

In order to measure the number of creative professionals, I use the most current *IAB-Regionalfile 1975-2004* scientific-use-file, which is published by the Nuremberg Research Data Centre FDZ (2008).[1,2] The IAB employee's data is given - with some exception - on administrative districts (NUTS3) and refers to workplace location.[3] It is a representative sample of 2 percent of all German employees, who are subject to compulsory insurance deductions, and includes approximately 21 million employment career histories. A disadvantage is that civil servants, freelancers and self-employed are not recorded in this employment sample.

---

1 Note that the analysis is based on data from the *IABS 1975-2004*. The data is accessible as a scientific-use-file, available from the Nuremberg Research Data Centre FDZ (2008) ("Die Datengrundlage dieses Beitrags bildet die faktisch anonymisierte IAB Beschäftigtenstichprobe (*IABS 1975 to 2004*). Der Datenzugang erfolgte über einen Scientific Use File, der vom Forschungsdatenzentrum der Bundesagentur für Arbeit im Institut für Arbeitsmarkt- und Berufsforschung zu beziehen ist.").

2 The "Institute of Employment Research" (IAB) is the research institute located within Germany's "Federal Employment Agency" and contributes to the employment discussion autonomously. The IAB has a statutory mandate to collect employment data.

3 In order to guarantee anonymity with the database, the administrative districts have to have at least 100,000 inhabitants, and when that is not the case, the FDZ (2008) aggregated them with districts surrounding them.

An advantage is that the IAB-Regionalfile includes data from social insurance provision for artists and publicists, the so-called *Künstlersozialkasse* (Social Welfare Fund for Artists) which also includes bohemian freelancers. The Social Welfare Fund for Artists is regarded as the most important insurance agency for employed and self-employed artists. Moreover, the samples time period is extraordinary long and the data census coherent in time. Employed agents subject to compulsory insurance deductions accounts for approximately 70 percent of the total labour force in Germany (Bundesagentur für Arbeit [Federal Employment Agency] 2007). In the *IAB-Regionalfile 1975-2004*, it is possible to identify 130 professional groups (by means of a three-digit code) and thereby identify detailed information on individuals income, nationality, or work place. A further advantage of this sample is the inclusion of the regional professional composition of the employed persons and, more importantly, the sample is representative for German employees. Furthermore, the work at hand benefits from high validity, sufficient reliability, and the relative up to date nature of the data (Drews 2008; Hamann et al. 2004).[4]

In the following, the process of data cleaning and preparation, as well as the variables used for the econometric model are described.

Data cleaning and preparation. In a first step, I selected the years 1977 up to 2004 and data for western German regions only (Berlin is also excluded).[5] The reporting date is December 31 of each year. I include only one observation for each employed individual per year (Drews et al. 2007). Since the individuals working in the creative sector often work with part-time labour contracts, I include both the group of part- and full-time employed individuals. I exclude all agents in apprenticeship. Moreover, I drop all observations which have no valid information on occupation, and all observations with missing information on region.

After the first data cleaning, the data show that around 10 percent of the observations have no information about the level of education in the education variable, with a total number of 10,932,559 observations. Given that the education variable suffers from a relatively large number of missing information, I impute values for missing education data in a second step by following the imputation procedure IP1 by Drews (2006) and Fitzenberger et al. (2005).

The education variable can take six different values which are (1) basic education (Hauptschule, Realschule), (2) basic education with a vocational training degree, (3) high school degree (Gymnasium), (4) high school degree and vocational training degree, (5) university

---

4 In mid 2011 a new and full version of the IAB-Regionalfile (SIAB, Sample of Integrated Labour Market Biographies) was set up, and includes data through 2008.

5 More information on the units of observation is provided below.

of applied science/technical college degree, and (6) university degree. According to the IP1 rule, I consider the highest educational degree reported for an individual. A further adjustment is that individuals below the age of 18 are considered as having no formal education (i.e. education 2-6). Another important aspect is the linkage between age and formal education. I do not extrapolate below a specific age limit (university 29 years, technical college 27 years, both vocational training and high school 23 years, high school only 21 years, and vocational education only 20 years). Another adjustment is the correction of individuals with missing education information who simultaneously have the employment status of skilled workers (*Facharbeiter*), foremen (*Polier*), and master craftsmen (*Meister*). Whenever I observe an employment status of skilled workers, foremen or master craftsmen together with no education information, I extrapolate the imputed information to that spell. Skilled workers, foremen, and master craftsmen are declared as having a vocational training degree. All further cases with missing information on education are deleted. For the time period 1977 to 2004, a total of 10,920,580 observations are obtained. Table 5.1 shows the distribution shares of the variables with and without the IP1 imputation procedure. The correlation between those two variables is 78 percent, and table 5.2 presents this correlation.

Table 5.1.: Distribution of the education variable with and without IP1 in percent (1977-04)

Education variables...	...without IP1	...with IP1
0. Missing	9.04	.
1. Basic eduction, no vocational education	19.49	19.38
2. Basic eduction with vocational education	61.70	67.76
3. Gymnasium, no vocational education	0.81	0.64
4. Gymnasium with vocational education	2.58	4.14
5. University of applied science	2.66	3.28
6. University	3.71	4.80
0-6. Missing-University	100	100

Notes: Number of observations=10,920,580.
Source: IABS Regionalfile 1975-2004, FDZ (2008), own calculations.

In the last step of data cleaning and preparation, I impute estimated wage values for censored values in the wage variable, by following the technique and the procedure worked out by Gartner (2005). That means wages below (*Geringfügigkeitsgrenze*) or above (*Beitrags-bemessungsgrenze*) a certain level are censored, because the wages are related to a specific contribution limit of the social security. This contribution limit differs over the years.

First, I deleted the wages below the contribution limit, since the employment sample only contains 20,258 observations with this characteristic. Second, I estimated the missing wages above the contribution limit by using a Tobit model formulated and distributed by Gartner (2005). I impute the estimated wages in Euro, before 1999 the Deutsche mark was used. The wages (day-to-day wage) are gross values. In the last step of data preparation, those 10,900,322 remained observations are aggregated to the level of 74 planning regions.

Table 5.2.: Correlation for the education variable with and without IP1 in percent (1977-04)

Variable	without IP1	with IP1
without IP1	100	
with IP1	77.9	100

Notes: Number of observations=10,920,580.
Source: IABS Regionalfile 1975-2004, FDZ (2008), own calculations.

Dependent variable. I analyse employment growth. The dependent variable $\triangle EMP$ is calculated by using absolute employment data for the intervals 1980-1986, 1989-1995, and 1998-2004. The growth rate is approximated by $growth_t = ln(variable_t) - ln(variable_{t-1})$. I use only natural logs (i.e. logs to the base e). With this specification, I follow Suedekum's (2006; 2008) or Glaeser et al. (1992) empirical work.

For research question 3, I add variables for the employment growth of the employed agents with technological creative ability (variable $\triangle TE$), agents with technological and economic creative ability, meaning the creative class, (variable $\triangle CC$), and employed high-skilled agents (variable $\triangle EDU$). Those variables are used in a further econometric application as dependent variables and shall capture the potential process of catching-up between cities and regions (Suedekum 2006, 2008). The dependent variable - total employment and sector specific growth - is connected to a set of explanatory variables, whereas the independent variables are assumed to be essential for the regression on the basis of the literature on the creative sector.

First, I report on some descriptive statistics. Figure 5.1 plots the correlation between the total employment and the total labour force for the three initial years 1980, 1986, and 1995 by 222 planning regions.[6] The correlation between those two variables is very high (99 percent): There is a strong relation between employment and labour force.

---

6 Note that on regional level, no data is available for the total labour force in 1977.

Accordingly, the data quality of the IAB-Regionalfile in relation to the data from the Regional Account VGR der Laender (2007)[7] seems to be valid and high.

The mean over the three intervals of the overall employment growth $\triangle EMP$ is 5.4 percent, for the growth of the creative sector $\triangle TE$ 12.4 percent, for Florida's creative class $\triangle CC$ 4.3 percent, and for high-skilled agents $\triangle EDU$ 19.9 percent (see table 5.6). A graphical comparison of these results is provided in figure 5.2, which indexes the development of total employment, the creative sector, Florida's creative class, and high-skilled employment for a cross-section of 222 regions.[8] Total employment has almost remained flat, while the number of high-skilled employed individuals has more than doubled through 2004. However, also the creative sector and Florida's creative class show a remarkable increase.

Figure 5.1.: Labour force and IABS employment sample

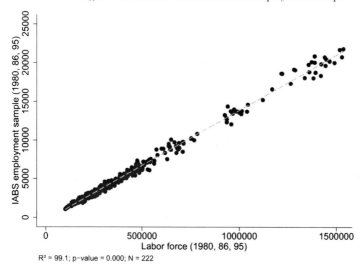

R² = 99.1; p−value = 0.000; N = 222

Source: IABS Regionalfile 1975-2004, FDZ (2008), own calculations

---

7 The 'Volkswirtschaftliche Gesamtrechnungen der Länder" (Regional Accounts VGR der Laender) provides a complete and consistent methodological and conceptual framework for measuring the economic activity on a regional level. The VGR der Laender is a working group of the regional statistical authorities.

8 Approximately 90 percent of the total employment worked full-time. Moreover, in the years 1977, 1986, and 1995, around 10 percent of bohemians worked part-time. In comparison only 4 percent of the part-time working employees are technological employees. Furthermore, around 14 percent of the employees working part-time had a low-skilled education (cf. table A.1.6 in the appendix).

Figure 5.2.: Total versus group specific employment development

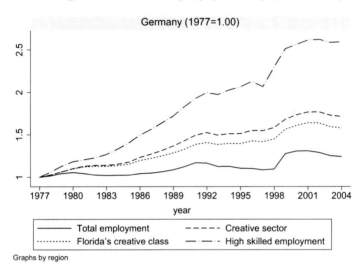

Source: IABS Regionalfile 1975-2004. FDZ (2008), own calculations

Variables for creative professionals and skill groups. For the purposes of measuring the creative sector, engineering, technical, scientific and IT professionals have been aggregated into a share of technological employees (variable TE, cf. table A.3 in the appendix and chapter 4). The group of technological employees is characterised as improving "technology in the line of business they pursue, and as a result, productivity and growth" (Murphy et al. 1991, 505). This group is considered to be highly creative and innovative, in other words, they have an ability for technological creativity. For the basic regression analysis, the initial shares of technological employees in 1977, 1986, and 1995 are considered. Furthermore, the second agent group of the creative sector, the bohemians (variable BOH), are included in the analysis as an independent variable. It is assumed that bohemians - agents working as artists, publishers, or audio engineers - are a location factor that increases economic dynamism and the local atmosphere. Bohemians themselves also produce economic outcome, according to the assumption. The initial share of bohemians in 1977, 1986, and 1995 are computed.

The alternative measure for the creative sector is the share of the creative class (variable CC) as defined by Florida (2002). The variable CC captures the technological and economic creative ability of agents. Once again, the bohemian agent group, BOH, is separately added into the regression analysis. The definition of the creative class is docu-

Table 5.3.: Summary of the creative sectors, creative class, and high-skilled agents labels

Human capital	Sector/Group	Agents with the ability of...	Variable
Creative (human) capital (i.e. creative professionals)	Creative sector	... technological creativity (i.e. technological employees)	*TE*
		... cultural creativity	*BOH*
	(Florida's) Creative class	... technological and economic creativity	*CC*
		... cultural creativity	*BOH*
Educational (human) capital	High-skilled agents	agents with an university degree	*EDU*

mented in table A.4 in the appendix. The group of the creative class is expected to have an effect on the overall employment growth. For the analysis, I took the initial share of the creative class 1977, 1986 and 1995. Alternatively, the third control measure is that of the share of high-skilled employment (variable *EDU*) (see also Table 5.3).[9]

Table 5.4 presents the correlation matrix using a cross-section of 222 (planning) regions for the different group-specific variables. It is obvious that the relative share of the creative class, *CC*, is relatively highly correlated with the share of employed agents with technological creative abilities (94.9 percent), the technological employees. This is not a surprise, since both definitions are strikingly similar. The match between the technological employees and bohemians is considerably smaller (52.1 percent) than the ratio between *CC* and *BOH* (0.636). Interesting is also the relatively high correlation between the share of high-skilled agents and the creative class (91.5 percent). In general, the employees from the creative sector and the creative class are better educated than the rest of the employees. For their part, bohemians tend to have more medium-skill education, and the technological and economic creative agents have high-skill education (cf. A.1.7 in the appendix).

Figure 5.3 shows the correlation between the natural log of wage and the share of the creative sector. The wage data measures productivity. The R^2 value is relatively high (68.5 percent in 1977, 72.7 percent in 1986, and 76.3 percent in 1995) which supports the result that the measure is valid and reliable for measuring the relation between productivity and technological creativity. The results are very similar for the correlation between the natural log of wages and the share of Florida's creative class (70.1 percent in 1977, 68.8 percent in 1986, and 76.4 percent in 1995) as well as between wage and the high-skilled

---

9 The differentiation in educational level is made between low-skilled (no vocational education, IAB-label 1 and 3), medium-skilled (with vocational education, IAB-label 2-4), and high-skilled (university, IAB-label 5 and 6).

Table 5.4.: Correlation between the different groups (1977, 86, 95)

Variable	TE	BOH	CC	EDU
Technological employees (TE)	1.000			
Bohemians (BOH)	0.521	1.000		
Creative class (CC)	0.949	0.636	1.000	
High-skilled employees (EDU)	0.873	0.650	0.915	1.000

Notes: Number of observations=222.
Source: IABS Regionalfile 1975-2004, FDZ (2008), own calculations.

employed agents (62.8 percent in 1977, 63.2 percent in 1986, and 74.1 percent in 1995).[10] In respect to the theory, there is a long-run relationsship between wage and employment.

All variables, the share of creative professionals (creative sector and creative class), and the share of high-skilled agents, are calculated on the basis of the employment data in the "IABS Regionalfile 1975-2004" from the FDZ (2008). Tables A.3 to A.5 in the annex give a detailed overview of all three employment groups.

Figure 5.3.: Creative sector and wage (1977, 86, 95)

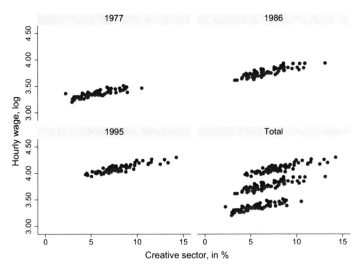

Notes: year 1977: R^2 = 68.48 percent, p-value=0.000, N=74; year 1986: R^2 = 72.67 percent, p-value=0.000, N=74; year 1995: R^2 = 76.32 percent, p-value=0.000, N=74
Source: IABS Regionalfile 1975-2004, FDZ (2008), own calculations

---

10 Cf. table A.2.1 and A.2.2 in the appendix.

Diversity. Jacobs (1969) suggests that professional diversity might contribute to the overall development of economies. Here the argument is that diverse professionals bring diverse knowledge backgrounds into the production process. In order to operationalise diversity, I measure the relative concentration of the creative sector among technological employees by using a Herfindahl-Hirschman-Index. $DIV_{it} = 1 - \sum_{k=1}^{k} s_{ikt}^2$, where s_{ikt} is the share of technological employees with profession k in region i in year t. This index thus takes only the diversity among technological employees into account (variable DIV_TE). Here, the diversity of bohemians is not considered. For the alternative, second definition of the creative sector (i.e. the creative class), I use a diversity measure for the creative class (variable DIV_CC), again the bohemians are excluded from the diversity index. Since the education variable has six different characteristics, I also construct a variable for the diversity by skill group (variable DIV_EDU).

In order to incorporate an additional measure of diversity, I include the share of employees who are not German (i.e. are citizens of another country, variable DIV). Due to data restrictions, the diversity index by nationality is only available from 1995 on. Since the correlation between employees by nationality and the share of employees with foreign nationality is more than 90 percent, I use this relative measure as a proxy to measure ethnic-cultural diversity. Ethnic-cultural diversity is assumed to be important in the knowledge creation process, assuming that more differentiated knowledge increases the possible combination of knowledge and knowledge networks (Audretsch et al. 2009; Florida 2002; Lee et al. 2004). In the econometric analysis, I took the share of foreign nationals for the years 1977, 1986, and 1995 into consideration. The share of employees with a foreign nationality was calculated with the *IABS Regionalfile 1975-2004* (FDZ 2008) data.

In the economics literature on entrepreneurship, there is a great deal of discussion over the use of polynomial functional forms, which take on U- or inverted U-shaped forms, in considering industrial diversity or industrial concentration (see, for instance, Fritsch and Slavtchev 2009). When using this technique, the slope is expected to change its sign. It would be possible to determine the optimum level of a relationship between the dependent and independent variable (see, for instance, Studenmund 2006; Wooldridge 2009). In the estimations, however, I do not consider polynomial forms for the diversity variables DIV_TE, DIV_CC, DIV_EDU, and DIV. Such a model would probably provide sensitive information on the optimum level of employed agents by nationality, however, the research aim is not to determine such an optimum. Second, in the empirical investigation I tested such a functional specification with the squared variable of DIV (DIV^2), DIV_TE (DIV_TE^2), DIV_CC (DIV_CC^2), and DIV_EDU (DIV_EDU^2). These specifications did not contribute to the overall fit (i.e. adjusted R^2).

Third, this functional form would further reduce the degrees of freedom, since the modeled relationship with a quadratic equation increases the number of coefficients.

Further control variables. Besides the creative professionals and the diversity measures as independent variables, I have included various control variables usually applied in employment growth regressions. Control variables for the employment size of the planning regions are added (variable EMP). I further use a variable for agglomerated regions in the initial years 1977, 1986, and 1995 (variable AGG). Agglomerated regions are regions which had more than 70 percent of Germany's regional mean of employment. Those are regions with an employment concentration above the 70th percentile. Since bohemians are assumed to be concentrated in highly agglomerated regions, I include the variable AGG in interaction with BOH (bohemians). Moreover, I add an interaction variable for AGG and DIV (AGG_DIV), AGG and TE (AGG_TE), AGG and CC (AGG_CC), as well as AGG and EDU (AGG_EDU).[11] Using this specification I can control for regional differences, since it is expected that higher shares of agents with technological creative abilities are concentrated in regions with high employment concentrations and agglomerative characteristics. This will influence the econometric results. Table 5.5 briefly describes the variable names and their abbreviations for the econometric model. Table 5.6 shows the summary statistics of the variables with their mean, standard deviation (Std. Dev.), minimum (Min.), and maximum (Max.).

Typical further controls such as the growth of the population, as presented in Glaeser (2008) for example, are not considered, because the direction of causality between population and employment growth is uncertain. Additionally, the relative size of total employment in the service sector is also not taken into account. In the economic literature, it is often argued that the service sector contributes to regional growth, since service businesses tend to bring out more employment than industrial production. Since the share of the service sector contains occupational groups of both Florida's creative class and the service sector, I exclude sector variables such as industrial production or the business sector to avoid possible multicollinearity problems. The initial share of wages is also further not included in the final regression model, since the wage variable caused multicollinearity problems with the variables TE, CC, and EDU. The causality linkage related to whether agents are attracted by high local wages or high local wages are caused by economic agents is furthermore technically unsolved. However, wage and employment are somehow in the long-run related.[12]

---

11 Cf. for the methodology and use of interaction variables, for instance, Studenmund (2006) or Wooldridge (2009).

12 Though human capital externalities are supposed to affect productivity level and not directly employment, it can be argued that changes in skill specific productivity levels have an impact on the growth

Table 5.5.: Variable descriptions

△EMP	Total employment growth
△TE	Technological employment growth
△CC	Florida's creative class growth
△EDU	Skill-based growth
TE	Share of technological employees
CC	Share of Florida's creative sector
EDU	Share of employees with university degree
BOH	Share of bohemians
DIV_TE	Diversity index of TE
DIV_CC	Diversity index of CC
DIV_EDU	Diversity index of EDU
DIV	Share of employees with other nationality than German
EMP	Log of total employment
AGG_TE	Interaction dummy of TE ...
AGG_CC	Interaction dummy of CC ...
AGG_EDU	Interaction dummy of EDU ...
AGG_BOH	Interaction dummy of BOH ...
AGG_DIV	Interaction dummy of DIV ...

Notes: ... and regions with more than the 70th percentiles of total employment (region=1, otherwise=0); Growth (△) for 1980-86, 89-95, 98-04; Control variables for 1977, 86, 95.

Units of observation. I concentrate for two reasons on Western Germany. First of all, I focus on the time period between 1977 and 2004, which means that the data includes a large period before the re-unification. For Eastern Germany, the data are only available from 1992 on. Secondly the economic, political, and social structure still remains different in Western and Eastern Germany. Therefore, it makes sense to focus only on Western Germany. The aggregation level is made up of so-called planning regions (*Raumordnungsregionen*), which are functional regions. There are 97 planning regions in Germany. 74 of these are located in Western Germany.[13] These functional regions are defined according to commuter flows. The bases for the establishment of these planning regions are administrative districts (NUTS3),[14] which aim to provide a consistent link to the statistical data of those districts.

of jobs (in the long-run). In particular, if wages are sticky moving downwards at the lower end of the income distribution a relative productivity decline of low-skilled labour should decrease low-skilled employment (Schlitte 2010).

13 See figure A.2.3 in the appendix.

14 NUTS comes from the French *nomenclature d'unités territoriales statistiques*, i.e. nomenclature of units for territorial statistics. It is a geocode standard for statistical purposes. NUTS3 reflect to a large extent the German districts (*Kreise*).

The administrative districts are effectively merged into planning regions according to function and their central locations (*Oberzentren*), with the exception of the Free Hanseatic City of Bremen (Federal State of Bremen) and the Free and Hanseatic City of Hamburg (Federal State of Hamburg).

Table 5.6.: Summary statistics

Variable	Mean	Std. Dev.	Min.	Max.
△EMP	0.054	0.076	-0.107	0.244
△TE	0.124	0.115	-0.150	0.833
△CC	0.043	0.086	-0.182	0.484
△EDU	0.199	0.113	-0.082	0.667
TE	0.067	0.022	0.022	0.142
CC	0.129	0.029	0.066	0.242
EDU	0.059	0.026	0.014	0.169
BOH	0.006	0.003	0.001	0.020
DIV_TE	0.899	0.013	0.813	0.919
DIV_CC	0.917	0.015	0.852	0.939
DIV_EDU	0.463	0.043	0.361	0.596
DIV	0.070	0.036	0.011	0.192
EMP	8.247	0.675	6.960	9.920
AGG_TE	0.025	0.041	0.000	0.142
AGG_CC	0.045	0.072	0.000	0.242
AGG_EDU	0.023	0.038	0.000	0.169
AGG_BOH	0.002	0.004	0.000	0.020
AGG_DIV	0.027	0.045	0.000	0.192

Number of observation: 222; number of groups 74
Panel variable planning region: strongly balanced
Time variable: year 1977 to 2004

Notes: Growth (△) for 1980-86, 89-95, 98-04; Control variables for 1977, 86, 95.
Source: IABS Regionalfile 1975-2004, FDZ (2008), own calculations.

Due to the fact that the administrative districts have to be seen complementary to their surroundings, it is an advantage to take functional planning regions into consideration. Since regions are not isolated, but are "part of a spatial economic network" (Nijkamp et al. 1993, 1), or as Tobler stated "Everything is related to everything else, but near things are more related than distant things" Tobler (1970, 236). The 74 Western German planning regions are also characterised by their political structure. In this case, the 74 planning regions lie within the 11 Federal States of Western Germany, with the exception of the city of Bremerhaven.[15] The weakness of the definition of the German planning regions is that

---

15 The City of Bremerhaven - which also belongs to the Federal State and Free Hanseatic City of Bremen
    - is sorted to the administrative district Wesermarsch and Cuxhaven (Federal State of Lower Saxony),

they do not account for modes of economic activities such as consumption. However. the above-mentioned 10.900.322 remaining micro-observations are aggregated to the regional level of 74 planning regions (*Raumordnungsregionen*). I am thus able to obtain three observations for each planning region (year 1977. 1986. 1995). and in consequence secure a total of 222 observations.

5.2. Regional distribution and development of creative professionals

This section will primarily supply an overview on the regional distribution of the creative sector (variable *TE* and *BOH*). Some results for Florida's creative class and the high-skilled agents are also presented. The maps (figure 5.4) and the descriptive statistic in tables A.1.8-A.1.10 in the appendix provide some evidence that helps to address research question 4. which inquires about the regional distribution of the creative sector. Furthermore. this section provides some tentative insights into the first part of research question 5(a). which asks whether agglomerated regions are places with a higher share of creative professionals than peripheral regions. In the following. the statistical maps. regional distribution and development of the creative sector are briefly presented.

Figure 5.4 maps the distribution of the share of technological employees (*TE*) by Germany's planning regions in 1977 and 2004. According to the results for 1977. the Bavarian planning region for Munich had the highest share of technological employees (10.5 percent). and the Bavarian planning region of Ingolstadt the lowest (2.2 percent). In 2004. the planning region Munich still led with a share of 15.7 percent. whereas the planning region Westmittelfranken had the lowest concentration of employed agents with technological creative ability (4.5 percent) of the 74 planning regions. Both in 1977 and 2004 the agglomerated planning regions of Starkenburg (Darmstadt. 8.5 and 14.0 percent). Stuttgart (8.9 and 14.3 percent) and Nuremberg (*Industrieregion Mittelfranken*. 8.9 and 12.8 percent) exhibited high shares of technological employees. which can be explained through the regional concentration of automotive and other export-oriented industries. Other agglomerated areas like the city of Hamburg (6.8 and 10.5 percent) and the northwestern city of Bremen (6.9 and 10.2 percent) had relatively high employment shares of technological employees in both 1977 and 2004. In general. there is a visible tendency toward technological employee concentration being located in the south of Germany.

Figure 5.4 also shows the spatial distribution of bohemians (*BOH*) in Germany. Excluding Berlin. the three biggest German cities Hamburg (1.4 percent). Cologne (1.3 percent). and

---

cf. also figure A.1 in the appendix.

Figure 5.4.: Regional distribution of the creative sector (1977, 04)

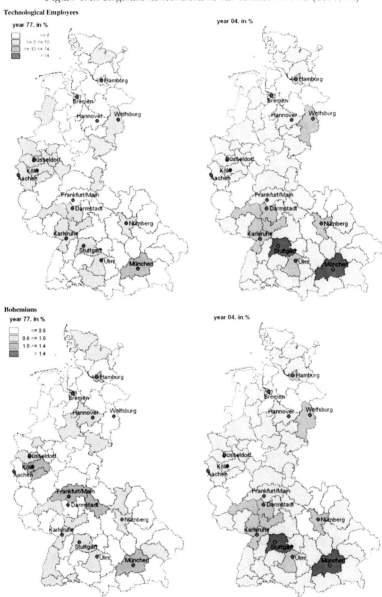

Munich (1.3 percent) had the highest shares of bohemians in 1977, but by 2004 Hamburg (1.9 percent) had lost its relatively dominant position, as the share of bohemians was higher in Munich (2.0 percent). In 2004, the central German city of Bonn had one of the highest shares of bohemians (1.3 percent), as well as the city of Frankfurt (1.1 percent). In 1977, eight regions had more than a 1 percent share of bohemians. Three regions had more than 1.5 percent. In 2004, twelve regions had between a 1 and 1.5 percent share of bohemians, whereas three regions had above a 1.5 percent share of bohemians. In general, between the years 1977 and 2004, the share of bohemians has increased.

Table A.1.8 in the appendix presents the statistics for the distribution of the creative sector by the variable agglomerated regions (AGG) for 1977 and 2004. The variable AGG measures the absolute employment concentration within a region. Those are regions with an employment concentration above the 70th percentile. In both years 1977 and 2004, table A.1.8 indicates that the highest relative concentration of technological employees can be found within the agglomerated regions (on average 69 percent in 1977 and 67 percent in 2004). This is also the case for the share of bohemians (on average 70 percent in 1977 and 70 percent in 2004). The growth rates are considerably different between both region types. In regions without a high employment concentration (AGG=0) the growth rate of TE was 16.7 percentage points and for BOH 1.6 percentage points higher. Tables A.1.9 and A.1.10 show the distribution of Florida's creative class and high-skilled agents. The growth rates are considerable high for the creative class (in mean 45.64 percent between 1977 and 2004). However, the dynamic was highest in regions with less employment concentration (AGG=0). The same results can be described for high-skilled agents. Interesting here is that the growth rate among low-skilled agents has been negative (-11.4 percent) for agglomerated regions ($AGG = 1$) between 1977 and 2004. The low-skilled agents has been replaced by more skilled agents (imperfect substitute). In less-agglomerated regions this growth rate has been positive (3 percent).

Figure 5.5 is a graph of the relation between the two region types $AGG = 1$ and $AGG = 0$. The above results can be confirmed. The creative sector, Florida's creative class, and the high-skilled agents are more concentrated in agglomerated regions than in less-agglomerated regions.

Figure 5.6 shows the relationship between the growth rate of technological employees between 1980 to 1986, 1989 to 1995, 1998 to 2004, and its related initial shares in 1977, 1986, and 1995. Those regions with relatively low shares of technological employees grow faster than those regions with relatively small shares of technological employees. Generally, there is a tendency for regions with lower shares of technological employees to catch-up to regions with higher shares. However, the three biggest German cities Munich, Hamburg, and Cologne had different dynamics. The growth rate of Munich was one of the highest (18.1 percent between 1980 and 1986; 2.1 percent between 1989 and 1995; 14.1 percent between 1998 and 2004). Munich's shares of technological employees was also the highest in 1977 (10.5 percent), 1986 (13.1 percent), and 1995 (14.2 percent). On the other hand, Cologne's growth rate was negative (-1.6 percent) between 1998 and 2004. The share of Cologne's technological employees was therefore one of the highest in Germany (1977: 8.5 percent; 1986: 9.6 percent; 1995: 10.2 percent).

Figure 5.5.: Share of creative sector, Florida's creative class, and high-skilled agents in a region type comparison (1977, 86, 95)

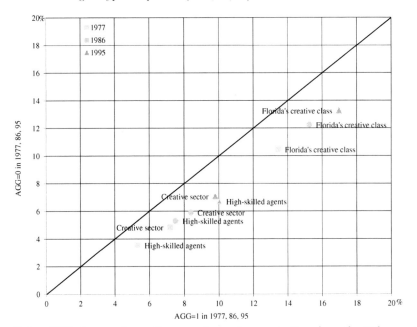

Notes: AGG=1 are regions with an employment concentration above the 70th percentile; AGG=1, 22 planning regions; AGG=0, 52 planning regions.
Source: IABS Regionalfile 1975-2004, FDZ (2008), own calculations.

Figure 5.7 presents the growth rate for the three intervals from 1980 to 1986, 1989 to 1995, and 1998 to 2004. Panel a of figure 5.7 shows the growth rates for the mean of Germany. In general, employment increased between 1980 and 2004. The growth rates for high-skilled agents were the highest. However, the growth levels of high-skilled agents decreased from one interval to the next interval, especially in the intervals from 1989 to 1995 and 1998 to 2004. The employment growth of TE was relatively stable between the three intervals. The growth of total employment thereby increased in the observed time period. In addition, the growth rates were considerably higher in non-agglomerated regions than in agglomerated regions (panels b and c).

Figure 5.6.: Growth of the creative sector (*TE*) (1980-86, 89-95, 98-04) in relation to their shares (1977, 86, 95)

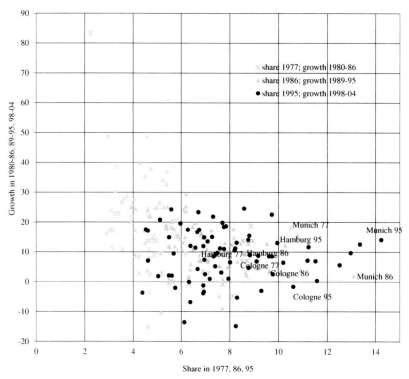

Notes: Growth is calculated by $growth_t = ln(variable_t) - ln(variable_{t-1})$.
Source: IABS Regionalfile 1975-2004, FDZ (2008), own calculations.

To sum up, the south of Germany is the most dynamic region in Germany. In the region of Munich the shares of *TE*, *CC*, and *EDU* have been the highest. Moreover, the highest concentration shares of the creative sector can be found within the regions with a high employment agglomeration (*AGG* = 1). On the other hand, growth rates have been higher in non-agglomerated regions (*AGG* = 0).

The next step is to investigate the interaction between total employment growth, group specific employment growth, and the shares of the creative sector, Florida's creative class, and employed agents with high-skilled education.

Figure 5.7.: Growth of the creative sector, Florida's creative class, and high-skilled agents by the *AGG* variable (1980-86, 89-95, 98-04)

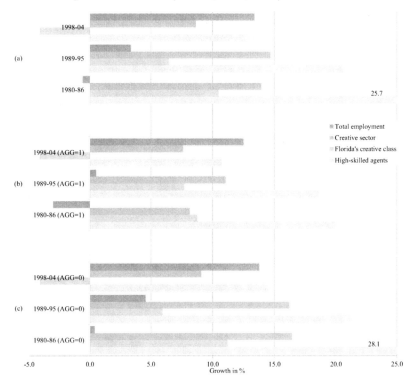

Notes: AGG=1 are regions with an employment concentration above the 70th percentile; AGG=1, 22 planning regions; AGG=0, 52 planningregions; Growth is calculated by $growth_t = ln(variable_t) - ln(variable_{t-1})$.
Source: IABS Regionalfile 1975-2004, FDZ (2008), own calculations.

5.3. Econometric model and specification

In a cross-section time-series analysis (panel analysis), I investigate whether the creative sector and diversity, more precisely the professional diversity and the diversity of agents by nationality, have any effect on the total employment growth for the subject time period from 1977 to 2004. I have further applied a few control variables that were ultimately important for employment growth. Thus the basic equation for the growth of total employment is:

$$
\begin{aligned}
\triangle EMP_{it} = {} & \beta_0 + \beta_1 TE_{it-3} + \beta_2 BOH_{it-3} \\
& + \beta_3 DIV\_TE_{it-3} + \beta_4 DIV_{it-3} + \beta_5 EMP_{it-3} \\
& + \beta_6 AGG\_BOH_{it-3} + \beta_7 AGG\_DIV_{it-3} \\
& + \beta_8 AGG\_TE_{it-3} + \epsilon_i \;,
\end{aligned}
\tag{5.1}
$$

where $\triangle EMP_{it}$ is the growth of the total employment in three intervals from 1980-1986, 1989-1995, and 1998-2004 in region i. With this computation, I obtain three observations for each planning region. There are 74 planning regions in Germany, resulting in a total of 222 observations.

Many economic situations imply non instantaneous relationships between the dependent and independent variables, in this case for instance employment and productivity or employment and bohemians, so that one ore more time lag variables need to be included. For this work, I do consider those to be lagged variables, although the literature on the creative sector does not provide explicit examples of market and hierarchy rigidities. However, it seems plausible that agents move to a particular city or region, and are willing to invest time before they expect positive economic growth. Using input variables with sufficiently time lags reduces concerns of reverse causality. Since the initial independent variables are lagged by three years (1977, 1986, and 1995), this problem is likely somewhat reduced. I further consider time and local area fixed effects in order to control for unobserved regional effects such as geographical features or effects which might be roughly constant over time (time-invariant), such as local cultural amenities or trust relations for example (see, for instance, Wooldridge 2009, and Chapter 3, the theoretical framework). This treatment is in line with the literature, and was used for instance by Suedekum (2006, 2008) in his research on human capital externalities and their impact on the growth of high-skilled employment.[16]

TE_{it-3} is the share of technological employees in 1977, 1986, and 1995, and BOH_{it-3} is the share of the bohemians in the initial years 1977, 1986, and 1995. DIV_TE_{it-3} is the diversity measure for the professional diversity, which is measured by the variety of technological employees in region i in year $t-3$. Once again I include the initial levels of the diversity measure for 1977, 1986, and 1995. DIV_{it-3} is the diversity of employees

---

16 Following Suedekum (2006, 2008). I have also tried various initial years, and other growth periods. For instance, I have also used two (and four) time periods, with longer (and shorter) time-lags. The empirical results have been relatively similar to those with three time periods and three years time-lags.

(share of employees with foreign nationality) for the three initial years $t - 3$. I control for the size of employment within the regions and cities (EMP). the variable is calculated by using the natural log of employment in the initial years 1977, 1986, and 1995. The last three variables AGG_BOH_{it-3}, AGG_DIV_{it-3}, and AGG_TE_{it-3} are interactions terms.

In general, the empirical results of equation 5.1 and also from the two following equations 5.2 and 5.3 are estimated both with and without the interaction terms. Furthermore, in order to appropriately model the relationship between the input and output variables, the input variables enter into the estimation with a time lag of three years. The error term is ϵ_{it}. The second basic equation is:

$$
\begin{aligned}
\triangle EMP_{it} = \; & \beta_0 + \beta_1 CC_{it-3} + \beta_2 BOH_{it-3} \\
& + \beta_3 DIV\_CC_{it-3} + \beta_4 DIV_{it-3} + \beta_5 EMP_{it-3} \\
& + \beta_6 AGG\_BOH_{it-3} + \beta_7 AGG\_DIV_{it-3} \\
& + \beta_8 AGG\_CC_{it-3} + \epsilon_i \;\;.,
\end{aligned}
\tag{5.2}
$$

where CC_{it-3} is the initial size of the creative class, and DIV_CC_{it-3} is the diversity of the creative class. Both variables are specified for the initial years 1977, 1986, and 1995. AGG_CC_{it-3} is an interaction term between CC_{it-3} and the region with high employment agglomeration AGG_{it-3}. The variables AGG_DIV_{it-3} and AGG_BOH_{it-3} are also interaction terms. The other variables are given by the estimation equation 5.1.

The third equation is:

$$
\begin{aligned}
\triangle EMP_{it} = \; & \beta_0 + \beta_1 EDU_{it-3} + \beta_2 BOH_{it-3} \\
& + \beta_3 DIV\_EDU_{it-3} + \beta_4 DIV_{it-3} + \beta_5 EMP_{it-3} \\
& + \beta_6 AGG\_BOH_{it-3} + \beta_7 AGG\_DIV_{it-3} \\
& + \beta_8 AGG\_EDU_{it-3} + \epsilon_i \;\;,
\end{aligned}
\tag{5.3}
$$

where EDU_{it-3} is the share of employed agents with a degree from a university of applied science or university (high-skilled) in region i and time $t - 3$. The other variables are specified as in model 5.1 above, with exception of the interaction terms DIV_EDU_{it-3} and AGG_EDU_{it-3}. The variable DIV_EDU_{it-3} measures the diversity of six different education degrees. AGG_EDU_{it-3} is an interaction term between AGG_{it-3}. the regional employment with more than a 70th percentiles level of employment, and EDU_{it-3} is the share of employees that are high-skilled agents.

All estimations were completed using fixed effects for each planning region and time period. With fixed effects it is possible to control for unobserved time-invariant explanatory variables. The number of observations is 222. or 74 observations for each year. and the panel variable planning region is strongly balanced.

5.4. Regression results

This section presents the regression results showing the effect of the creative sector. Florida's creative class. and the high-skilled employed agents on employment growth in Germany. I have divided this section into two subsections in order to separately present the estimation results on the total employment growth (section 5.4.1) and on group specific employment growth (section 5.4.2). The interpretations and their implications are discussed in detail in chapter 6.

Recall that chapter 4 presented six hypotheses that have been developed. Hypotheses 1 and 2 (research question 1) state that the share of creative professionals and the share of bohemians. respectively. contribute to general employment growth. They expect positive values for the contribution of the creative sector.

Hypothesis 3 (research question 2) theorised that the diversity of economic agents as measured by creative professionals' diversity is positively linked to employment growth. For this. a converted Herfindahl-Hirschman-Index is applied. The fourth hypothesis (research question 2) is that the diversity of economic agents, their ethnic-cultural diversity as approximated by the share of employees with foreign nationality. is positively linked to employment growth. Once again a positive coefficient is expected. If the coefficients are negatively significant. the result would then be that clustering is of importance for employment growth (see. for example. Glaeser et al. 1992; Porter 1998). Since there are conflicting hypotheses about the expected values of coefficients, a two-sided test is generally used to analyse the results ($H_0 : \beta_k = 0$ and $H_A : \beta_k \neq 0$) (see section 5.4.2).[17]

Hypotheses 5 and 6 (research question 3) state that the initial share of the creative professionals and bohemians affect the growth rate of the creative sector. If the value is negative for the creative sector a catching-up between the regions has to be assumed. Otherwise. the interpretation would be is that further polarisation is in process. Once again. a two-sided test is used ($H_0 : \beta_k = 0$ and $H_A : \beta_k \neq 0$).

---

17 There are two categories for using two-sided tests. First, a two-sided test is used whether "an estimated coefficient is significantly different from zero". Second, a two-sided test is applied whether "an estimated coefficient is significantly different from a specific nonzero value" (Studenmund 2006, 135).

5.4.1. Total employment effects

The panel is estimated with a fixed effects estimator (FE). Using this technique it is possible to consider unobserved effects. Since each planning region has its own time-independent characteristics that may or may not influence the predictor variables, the FE model is used as a control for this. However, the planning region's error term and the constant should not correlate with each other. When they correlate, the fixed effects model is not adequate. In that case, I would re-estimate the relationship with a random effects model (RE), which postulates that I have "good" control variables and that the unobserved effects are not correlated with the independent variables (see, for instance, Wooldridge 2009).

Having used a Hausman test to determine whether the error terms are correlated with the regressor, I conclude that the fixed effects estimator is adequate for all three equations (5.1-5.3). The level of significance for each is smaller than 5 percent. I also tested for random effects with a Breusch-Pagan-Lagrange multiplier (LM), which tests whether the variance across the planning regions is zero (null hypothesis). I conclude that the random effects estimator is not appropriate for all three equations (5.1-5.3). Furthermore, they are tested whether time fixed effects and fixed effects for entities are needed. Both are joint tests to see if dummies for all years and all entities are equal to zero. It is concluded from the joint test that fixed effects are needed. Table A.3.1 in the appendix documents the test results for all three estimation equations. Additional test diagnostics are presented in the appendix, i.e. testing for cross-sectional dependence and heteroscedasticity. The results of the cross-sectional dependence (CD) of Pesaran's test indicate substantial CD in the errors both of the estimation equations 5.1 and 5.2. These errors may arise because of the presence of neighbourhood effects. The Pesaran's test fails to reject the null hypothesis in the estimation model for the high-skilled agents (**Definition 3**). Calculating Pesaran's average absolute values, however, results in a high value (correlation is 0.657). Hence, there is enough evidence suggesting the presence of CD in the estimation of equation (5.3). De Hoyos and Sarafidis (2006), but also Hoechle (2007), alternatively suggest calculating the standard errors (SE) with Driscoll-Kraay SE, correcting for CD. More-over, the Driscoll-Kraay SE produces heteroscedasticity and autocorrelation-consistent SE "that are robust to general forms of spatial and temporal dependence" (Driscoll and Kraay 1995, 282). In following, I use the Driscoll-Kraay SE in the estimations.

Creative sector: Definition 1. Column 1 and 2 present the results for the creative sector (table 5.7). The first column presents the estimation results for equation 5.1. The second column shows the results for a re-estimated equation 5.1. without the interaction variable AGG_*_{it-3}. First of all, as reflected in the R^2 of table 5.6, the overall fit of the estimation is good (62 percent).

Table 5.7.: Total employment growth (1980-86, 89-95, 98-04)

Variable	Definition 1		Definition 2		Definition 3	
			Dependent variable: $\triangle$EMP			
TE	3.587**	3.348**	.	.	.	.
	(0.091)	(0.103)				
CC	.	.	2.409**	2.240**	.	.
			(0.058)	(0.093)		
EDU	.	.	.	.	4.494**	4.259**
					(0.151)	(0.078)
BOH	12.082**	10.682**	12.748**	10.968**	2.671**	1.116
	(1.440)	(0.877)	(1.757)	(1.259)	(0.829)	(1.426)
DIV_TE	1.190**	1.290**	.	.	.	.
	(0.187)	(0.201)				
DIV_CC	.	.	0.795*	0.944**	.	.
			(0.325)	(0.334)		
DIV_EDU	.	.	.	.	-1.374**	-1.524**
					(0.127)	(0.120)
DIV	1.551**	1.684**	1.723**	1.855**	2.079**	2.180**
	(0.218)	(0.238)	(0.310)	(0.287)	(0.101)	(0.061)
EMP	0.034	0.041	0.098†	0.099†	-0.051	-0.033
	(0.044)	(0.044)	(0.056)	(0.055)	(0.031)	(0.028)
AGG_TE	-0.335	.	.	.	.	.
	(0.224)					
AGG_CC	.	.	0.056	.	.	.
			(0.151)			
AGG_EDU	.	.	.	.	-0.585**	.
					(0.211)	
AGG_BOH	-4.492	.	-9.260**	.	-2.557	.
	(3.377)		(2.446)		(3.156)	
AGG_DIV	0.453**	.	0.567*	.	0.395**	.
	(0.133)		(0.244)		(0.127)	
Constant	-1.715**	-1.853**	-1.996**	-2.120**	0.692**	0.621**
	(0.223)	(0.248)	(0.179)	(0.224)	(0.238)	(0.204)

NOB: 222; Local area fixed effect: YES; time period fixed effect: YES

| R^2 | 62.22% | 61.88% | 60.93% | 60.48% | 80.35% | 79.76% |

Notes: Significance levels= †: 10%, *: 5%, **: 1%; Driscoll-Kraay standard errors in parentheses; Control variables for 1977, 1986, 1995.
Source: IABS Regionalfile 1975-2004, FDZ (2008), own calculations.

The creative sector, which consists of the agents employed in the field of technological creativity and agents employed as bohemians, contributes on a different scale to total employment growth. The coefficient of the initial share of technological employees (TE_{it-3}) is highly significant. The hypothesis 1 (for β_1, $Reject\ H_0\ if\ |39.42| > 1.86$) can therefore be rejected. It can be concluded that the agents with technological creative abilities do force total employment growth. Holding the other variables constant, a one unit increase in TE_{it-3} will lead to a 3.6 percent change in (future) total employment.

The effect of the initial share of bohemians, BOH_{it-3}, on total employment growth is also significant at every level. It is therefore concluded that bohemians matter in the overall context of urban and regional employment growth, and the null hypothesis can be rejected (for β_2, $Reject\ H_0\ if\ |8.39| > 1.86$). A one unit increase in BOH_{it-3} leads to a 12 percent change in (futures) employment.

For DIV_TE_{it-3} the coefficient is positive and significant at the 1 percent level (1.190). I can conclude that diversity matters, and the null hypothesis can be rejected (for β_3, $Reject\ H_0\ if\ |6.36| > 1.86$). Hypothesis 4 is that the ethnic-cultural diversity (DIV_{it-3}) is positively linked to total employment growth. Its coefficient is significant at any significance level (1.551). The null hypothesis for the fourth assumption, that ethnic-cultural diversity has no effect on employment growth, can be rejected (for β_4, $Reject\ H_0\ if\ |7.08| > 1.86$). Concluding results are that the diverse occupational composition of the creative sector and labour is linked to total employment growth.

The coefficient of the interaction term AGG_DIV_{it-3} is also positive and significant (0.453). All other coefficients of the variables AGG_TE_{it-3}, AGG_BOH_{it-3}, and EMP_{it-3} are insignificant.

Florida's creative sector: Definition 2. Column 3 and 4 present the estimation results for Florida's creative class. Again, the number of observations is 222 and the Driscoll-Kraay standard errors are reported in parentheses. As reflected in the R-squared of table 5.7, the overall fit of the fixed effect regression is 61 percent, the result is similar to that of **Definition 1**.

In general, the results indicate the same signs as for the above econometric equation (5.1) The coefficient of the share of the creative class (CC_{it-3}) is positively significant on total employment ($\triangle EMP_{it}$) (2.409). The coefficient of BOH_{it-3} is positive and significant at the 1 percent level (12.748).

Once again, the coefficient of the diversity of economic agents, that is DIV_CC_{it-3}, is positive and significant at the 5 percent level (0.795). This result is compatible with the hypothesis that the diversity of Florida's creative class - here measured by a Herfindahl-Hirschman-Index - is of importance for employment growth. The coefficient of ethnic-cultural diversity (DIV_{it-3}) is positively significant at the 1 percent level (1.723).

The share of the agents employed as bohemians, BOH_{it-3}, in interaction with the AGG_{it-3} variable is negatively significant at the 1 percent level (-9.260). The variable EMP_{it-3} is marginally positively significant at the 10 percent level (0.098). However, the coefficient of AGG_CC_{it-3}, the interaction variable between AGG_{it-3} and CC_{it-3}, is not significant.

High-skilled agents: Definition 3. The estimation results for the employed high-skilled agents are highlighted in column 5 and 6 of table 5.7. The R^2 of the FE estimation is around 80 percent. At a glance, the results are not very different from the creative sector and its alternative of the creative class.

The coefficient of the share of high-skilled agents (EDU_{it-3}) is positive and highly significant at the 1 percent level (4.494). The BOH variable is positive and significant at the 1 percent level, with a coefficient of 2.671. The coefficient of the variable DIV_EDU_{it-3} is negative at the significance level of 1 percent (-1.374), which indicates the importance of a relatively high concentration of a non-diversified group of educated agents. In contrast, the coefficient DIV_{it-3} is positively significant (2.079). The interaction variable between the share of high-skilled agents EDU_{it-3} and the agglomerated regions AGG_{it-3} is negatively significant at the 1 percent level, and the coefficient is -0.585. Moreover, the result for the interaction variable AGG_EDU_{it-3} is negatively correlated with $\triangle EMP_{it}$, the total employment growth (-0.585). All other coefficients are insignificant.

A comparison of the estimated results of column 6 - i.e. the re-estimation of equation 5.3 without the interaction term AGG_*_{it-3} - with column 5, reveals that the estimations indicate in the same direction.

5.4.2. Group specific employment effects

Once again, I estimate all equations 5.1 to 5.3 with the three dependent variables growth in technological employees $\triangle TE_{it}$, growth of Florida's creative class $\triangle CC_{it}$, and growth of employed high-skilled agents $\triangle EDU_{it}$.[18] I analyse these employment specific growth rates separately to investigate a potential convergence or divergence between the regions. Again I split up the observations in three intervals and compute the growth rates for 1980-1986, 1989-1995, and 1998-2004. Control variables for the three intervals are computed for 1977, 1986, and 1995. I test the three equations in a panel model.

---

18 The three equations with dependent variables are:

$$\triangle TE_{it} = \beta_0 + \beta_1 TE_{it-3} + \beta_2 BOH_{it-3} \\ + \beta_3 DIV\_TE_{it-3} + \beta_4 DIV_{it-3} + \beta_5 EMP_{it-3} \\ + \beta_6 AGG\_TE_{it-3} + \beta_7 AGG\_BOH_{it-3} \\ + \beta_8 AGG\_DIV_{it-3} + \epsilon_i$$

$$\triangle CC_{it} = \beta_0 + \beta_1 CC_{it-3} + \beta_2 BOH_{it-3} \\ + \beta_3 DIV\_CC_{it-3} + \beta_4 DIV_{it-3} + \beta_5 EMP_{it-3} \\ + \beta_6 AGG\_CC_{it-3} + ... + \epsilon_i$$

, and

$$\triangle EDU_{it} = \beta_0 + \beta_1 EDU_{it-3} + \beta_2 BOH_{it-3} \\ + \beta_3 DIV\_EDU_{it-3} + ... + \epsilon_i$$

In a first test, I check whether the error terms are correlated with the regressor. Table A.3.2 in the appendix documents the test results. The tests are calculated with a joint test on significance, a Breusch-Pagan-Lagrange multiplier (LM), and the Hausman test. With the exception of the Breusch-Pagan-Lagrange multiplier for the estimation model of **Definition 1** (prob>chi2 = 0.112), all results indicate that the fixed effects (FE) model is appropriate. Furthermore, the CD test of Pesaran's indicates cross-sectional dependence between the (planning) regions. The average absolute values are also regarded as very high (0.633, 0.650, 0.638) (for further methodology, see, Hoechle 2007). I therefore calibrated the standard errors with Driscoll-Kraay standard errors that are robust to cross-sectional dependence; moreover, the Driscoll-Kraay SE estimates are heteroscedasticity and autocorrelation consistent.

Creative sector: Definition 1. The results are presented in table 5.8. The overall fit of the FE estimator is around 30 percent. The variable of interest, TE_{it-3}, is negatively correlated with the growth in technological employment, and, the coefficient is significant at the 1 percent level (-3.898). TE_{it-3} significantly reduces the growth of the same employment group (i.e. ΔTE_{it}). Hypothesis 5 is therefore rejected, since for β_5, $Reject\ H_0\ if\ |12.07| > 1.86$.

BOH_{it-3} itself is negatively significant at the 1 percent level (-4.798). Regarding hypothesis 6, I can reject the null hypothesis, because the results are highly negatively significant (for β_6, $Reject\ H_0\ if\ |9.87| > 1.86$). In Germany's mean, bohemians reduce the growth rate of TE_{it-3}. The diversity among TE_{it-3} (DIV_TE_{it-3}) positively affects the growth of ΔTE_{it}. The coefficient is significant at the 1 percent level (3.059). The coefficient of the variable DIV_{it-3} is negative and highly significant (-0.466).

The interaction variable between the highly agglomerated regions - here calculated by the regional labour market size - and the initial share of technological employees AGG_TE_{it-3}, the coefficient is positively significant (0.707). Interestingly, the interaction variable AGG_BOH_{it-3} is also positively significant and the coefficient is very high (27.782). The regional concentration of bohemians within agglomerated regions positively influences the growth rate of agents with technological creative abilities. A one unit increase in bohemians in the initial years, BOH_{it-3} results in a 27.8 percent change in technological employees.

Table 5.8.: Group specific employment growth (1980-86, 89-95, 98-04)

Variable	ΔTE (Definition 1)		ΔCC (Def. 2)		ΔEDU (Def. 3)	
	Dependent variable					
TE	-3.898**	-2.948**	.	.	.	.
	(0.323)	(0.366)				
CC		.	-3.436**	-2.838**	.	.
			(0.058)	(0.104)		
EDU	.	.	.	.	-2.997**	-2.632**
					(0.177)	(0.149)
BOH	-4.798**	2.519†	-	-7.165**	1.176	5.268**
	(0.486)	(1.319)	12.351**	(1.286)	(0.929)	(0.334)
			(0.997)			
DIV_TE	3.059**	2.563**	.	.	.	.
	(0.448)	(0.546)				
DIV_CC	.	.	0.226	-0.316	.	.
			(0.266)	(0.244)		
DIV_EDU	.	.	.	.	-0.210	0.108
					(0.224)	(0.185)
DIV	-0.466**	-0.736**	-1.247**	-1.580**	0.468**	-0.026
	(0.139)	(0.241)	(0.239)	(0.219)	(0.148)	(0.115)
EMP	-0.221**	-0.242**	-0.285**	-0.283**	-0.245**	-0.272**
	(0.076)	(0.067)	(0.068)	(0.062)	(0.022)	(0.005)
AGG_TE	0.707**	.	.	.	.	.
	(0.054)					
AGG_CC	.	.	0.218**	.	.	.
			(0.078)			
AGG_EDU	.	.	.	.	0.740*	.
					(0.279)	
AGG_BOH	27.782**	.	23.926**	.	14.079**	.
	(3.198)		(0.798)		(3.295)	
AGG_DIV	-1.097**	.	-1.433**	.	-1.740**	.
	(0.257)		(0.128)		(0.076)	
Constant	-0.538	0.047	2.766**	3.193**	2.446**	2.515**
	(0.808)	(0.853)	(0.392)	(0.277)	(0.078)	(0.091)
R²	31.83%	26.99%	72.26%	68.98%	34.76%	33.1%

NOB: 222; Local area fixed effect: YES; time period fixed effect: YES

Notes: Significance levels= †: 10%, *: 5%, **: 1%; Driscoll-Kraay standard errors in parentheses; Control variables for 1977, 1986, 1995.
Source: IABS Regionalfile 1975-2004, FDZ (2008), own calculations.

Florida's creative class: Definition 2. The results from the estimation of the growth rate for the creative class go hand in hand with the above results on the creative sector. Nonetheless, the overall fit is much higher (72 percent). CC_{it-3}, that is the share of Florida's creative class, is negatively correlated with the growth rate of the creative class, $\triangle CC$. As stated however, the results are consistent with the result of the first definition. The coefficient is significant at the 1 percent level (-3.436). Also the result for the bohemian variable (BOH_{it-3}) is negatively significant (-12.351).

The ethnic-cultural diversity (DIV_{it-3}) is negatively significant at the 1 percent level (-1.247). The result for DIV_CC_{it-3} is insignificant. Contrary to the variable CC_{it-3}, the interaction variable AGG_CC_{it-3} is positively correlated with the growth of Florida's creative class and the coefficients are significant at the 1 percent level (0.218). Again the bohemian variable in interaction with the variable for the agglomerated regions (AGG_BOH_{it-3}) is positively significant and its coefficient is very high (23.926). Comparing the results of column 3 with the estimation that was completed without the interaction variables AGG_*_{it-3} (column 4, table 5.9), the coefficients' signs and significance levels indicate in the same direction.

High-skilled agents: Definition 3. Table 5.8 also presents the estimation results for the initial share of employed high-skilled agents on the growth of the employed high-skilled agents, $\triangle EDU$, with the Driscoll-Kraay standard errors are reported in parentheses. The overall fit is 35 percent which is in line with the FE models on $\triangle TE$ (cf. column 1 and 2). The results do not differ greatly from the econometric results of equations 5.1 and 5.2. Once again, the coefficient for the initial share of employed agents with more education, EDU_{it-3}, is negative and significant at the 1 percent level (-2.997). The share of bohemians BOH_{it-3} is positively correlated, but insignificant.

The variable DIV_EDU_{it-3} is also insignificant. The result of the employed agents with a foreign nationality, DIV_{it-3}, on the growth of the employed high-skilled agents differs in some aspects from the creative sector and its alternative definition, Florida's creative class. The coefficient is positive and highly significant at the 1 percent level (0.468).

Once again the interaction term between the employed high-skilled agents and the agglomerated regions ($AGG = 1$) is significant and positive, here at the 5 percent level (0.740) which indicates a further divergence process between the regions. The variable AGG_BOH_{it-3} is positively correlated and highly significant with $\triangle EDU$. Its coefficient is 14.079.

5.5. Interim summary

Table 5.9 summarises the outcome of the estimations for the six hypotheses. The three different employment groups, the technological employees TE_{it-3} (β_1), and also the two (control) definitions. Florida's creative class CC_{it-3} and the employed high-skilled agents EDU_{it-3}, are all linked to total employment growth.

Table 5.9.: Summary of the results for the creative sector in comparison with the two (control) definitions

Research Question	(1)		(2)		(3)	
Definition 1: Creative sector						
Hypothesis	β_1	β_2	β_3	β_4	β_5	β_6
Expected sign	+	+	+/-	+/-	+/-	+/-
Outcome	3.587	12.082	1.190	1.551	-3.898	-4.798
Significance level	**	**	**	**	**	**
Definition 2: Florida's creative class						
Outcome	2.409	12.748	0.795	1.723	-3.436	-12.351
Significance level	**	**	*	**	**	**
Definition 3: High-skilled agents						
Outcome	4.494	2.671	-1.374	2.079	-2.997	1.176
Significance level	**	**	**	**	**	

Notes: Significance levels= †: 10%, *: 5%, **: 1%; growth 1980-86, 89-95, 98-04; Control variables for 1977, 1986, 1995.
Source: IABS Regionalfile 1975-2004, FDZ (2008), own calculations.

However, the result for TE_{it-3} is highly significant at the 1 percent level. The coefficient for the initial level of BOH_{it-3} (β_2) is further positively significant. Interesting is also the result for the diversity measures DIV_TE_{it-3} (β_3), the coefficient is positively significant at the 1 percent level. In contrast to the two alternative definitions, the empirical findings here are at odds: DIV_CC_{it-3} shows the same result as the creative sector, but, the coefficient for the diversity of employees' educations DIV_EDU_{it-3} is negatively significant. However, DIV_{it-3} (β_4), the ethnic-cultural diversity, has a positive and highly significant coefficient (1.551).

Furthermore, the estimations show that the creative sector (i.e. TE_{it-3}) is also linked to its group specific employment growth $\triangle TE_{it}$ (β_5). The coefficient is negative and significant at the 1 percent level. Also the results for BOH_{it-3} on the group specific employment growth $\triangle TE_{it}$ is negatively significant (β_6). In contrast, these results vary greatly depending on whether we focus on the interaction variables AGG_TE_{it-3} and AGG_BOH_{it-3}. The estimations for these variables are positive and highly significant at the 1 percent level. The coefficient of the variable AGG_BOH_{it-3} is, moreover, very high (27.782). In chapter 6, the results are intepreted and discussed.

6. Implications and conclusions

This chapter discusses the implications of the empirical results for the theory. The conclusions drawn from the empirical work on the creative sector are of importance for policy and the policy case study. This chapter is divided into two sections, the first of which discusses the implications of the empirical findings (section 6.1), and the second, the conclusions we can draw from them (section 6.2). Section 6.1 is further separated into five sub-sections, which are ordered according to and discuss the hypothesis (1-6) and research questions (1-3) raised in this thesis.

Using IABS micro-data for the period from 1977 to 2004, the applied cross-section times series models with time-lags provide evidence that the effect of the agents of the creative sector (**Definition 1**), alternatively Florida's creative class (**Definition 2**) as well as the employed high-skilled agents (**Definition 3**) can explain total and sector specific employment growth in German regions. However, as shown in the following discussion the results, this explanatory ability depends on the size of the regions' employment market. Moreover, the result for the diverse composition of the creative sector, and also for the diversity of the creative class, provide evidence that occupational diversity is of importance for regional employment growth. The results of the estimations provide some further evidence for the debate on whether ethnic-cultural diversity has an impact on employment growth.

6.1. Implications

This work previously developed six hypotheses. Hypotheses 1 and 2 (research question 1) argued that the share of creative professionals and the share of bohemians positively contribute to general employment growth. Hypothesis 3 (research question 2) posited that the diversity of economic agents as measured by creative professionals' diversity is positively linked to employment growth. Hypothesis 4 (research question 2) theorised that the diversity of economic agents as indicated by their ethnic-cultural diversity is positively linked to employment growth.

Hypotheses 5 and 6 (research question 3) postulated that the initial share of the creative professionals and bohemians affect (positively or negatively) the growth rate of the creative sector.

Research question 1, hypothesis 1.   Agents with an ability for technological creativity (TE) contribute essential to total employment growth. The explanation for this results is that the number of creative professionals has, on the whole, seen disproportionate growth in the last decades. TE generates further employment, because this sector is related to other industries, such as service sectors, and is integrated into production chains and processes.[1] It can moreover be assumed that agents with technological creative abilities foster creative processes, contributing innovation, which can lead to further employment growth. The group of those technological employees is therefore fundamentally related to improving technology, production, and processes which result in productivity and (employment) growth.

Research question 1, hypothesis 2.   One explanation for a region's ability to attract those technological employees are the presence of unique local conditions and the value of local cultural amenities. Likewise, the competitiveness of regions lay in their ability to attract new economic agents and businesses rich in creative professionals. However, economic agents working in fields of cultural amenities are bohemians. They are supposed to create new products, to have an effect on taste, and to give impulse to production (product variety and externality). The empirical results generally suggest that bohemians (BOH) are positively related to total employment growth. The interpretation of this result is that employment is attracted by local cultural amenities, and bohemians themselves contribute to theses amenities through cultural-related products and services. This result confirms Florida's (2002) assumption that cultural input has a positive effect on economic growth.

Research question 2, hypothesis 3.   The diversity of technological employees DIV_TE is positively significant on total employment growth. This indicates the importance of diversity. The reason for this being that labour market pooling in the creative sector, but with different creative professions, raises the probability for externalities. Moreover, the assumption is that the relative clustering (or pooling) of the creative sectors in highly agglomerated regions increases the probability of positive (knowledge) externalities. This assumption is consistent with the definition of cities. First, cities are marked by the absence of physical space between agents and firms. Importantly, cities also concentrate

---

1 For further discussion on the linkages of the creative sector, see, for instance, Ye and Yin (2007).

a (minimum of a) critical mass of economic agents at one single place. High absolute numbers of creative professionals are fundamental for production processes and chains. This critical mass forces the sharing of (tacit) knowledge and local networks, but also encourages the diversification of firm's activities (i.e. diversifying behavior of firm acting). For both, it is neither possible to number the strength of such an external effect nor to quantify the minimum critical mass.[2] However, the empirical result is that diversity - that is the diverse composition of the technological creative agents - and not the clustering of one specific creative profession (Jacobs versus Porter or Marshall externalities), matters for total employment growth.

At a glance, these results appear to contradict the ideas and theories presented by, for instance, Marshall (1920a) or Porter (1998): Both underline the importance of employment pooling and branch clustering. However, the empirical findings show that the creative professionals are regionally pooled and diverse in their occupational composition. This has important consequences for economic and urban policies, since cluster strategies or complex networks and regional innovation systems are very often relevant to policy makers. The results suggest that strategies are most successful for clustered but diverse creative professionals (i.e. in its composition).

Alternatively, the estimation results show for the third definition that the clustering of high-skilled agents is of importance to the growth of employment (DIV_EDU). The coefficient of DIV_EDU is negatively significant; this indicates that the relative concentration of one specific knowledge group matters to total employment growth. One interpretation could be that more general (educational or school) knowledge is of importance for production and working processes. This is different from branch clustering, where specific, but diverse knowledge contributes to production.[3] Another interpretation would be that a specific knowledge group is statistically overrepresented in the empirical analysis, which is leading to measurement bias.

Research question 2, hypothesis 4. The findings further suggest that ethnic-cultural diversity (DIV) positively affects employment growth. The assumption is that productivity depends not only on the share of the creative agents, but that it also depends on the diversity of economic agents.

One interpretation is that diverse agents foster the combination and transmission of new ideas. New , more important, culturally-related knowledge is seen as a pre-requisite for

---

2 Elsner and Heinrich also discuss the "critical masses" of coordinated agents in a framework of a "meso" group in socio-economic areas as clusters or networks (Elsner and Heinrich 2009).

3 Branch clusters help to develop stable interactions between different economic agents, while this stable interaction connects single agents and enforces the sharing of expectations, trust, and knowledge between agents. See, for instance, Elsner (2004) and Elsner (2005).

the generation of new products. Another interpretation is that economic agents that decide to migrate will be strongly attracted to open regions and cities. Low entry barriers for economic agents are worthwhile, since agents can integrate themselves more quickly into markets if barriers (for instance, forms of social barriers and arrangements) are low.

Research question 3, hypothesis 5. It is worth recalling, that the theoretical model for research question 3 helped to explain whether the creative sector contributes to general employment growth, but in particular to sector specific employment growth. This model explains the self-reinforcing effect of employment in regions that already have high shares of the creative sector.

The empirical results show that the initial share of the creative sector retains a negative effect on the growth rate of the creative sector (TE on $\triangle TE$). In consequence, the assumption of convergence between the regions turns out to be positive. Regions with lower shares of the creative sector are catching up to regions with higher shares of the creative sector. The effect in relation to hypothesis 1 is as follows: Large shares of creative professionals lead to an increase in total employment, but it reduces the growth of the same employment group: The growth in total employment overwhelms the decline in creative professionals.

In contrast, for the growth rate of TE on $\triangle TE$, the results indicate that there is a significant divergence between the two region types (i.e. employment agglomerated (AGG) and less employment agglomerated). Based on the theory, the empirical results suggest that externalities are large enough to reinforce the group specific employment concentration in agglomerated regions. Productivity gains through knowledge spillovers may leverage wages and then average levels of creative (human) capital; this ongoing concentration may increase productivity (Rauch 1993). This will again bring about the accumulation of more creative agents. I conclude therefore that there is a self-reinforcing process within already highly agglomerated regions. The interpretation can be that other, less aggregated regions will continue to catch-up to the German mean. The polarisation of creative professionals depends in consequence on the spatial type of observation (agglomerated versus less agglomerated regions). This further pooling of creative professionals will therefore only increase in a few single regions (for example, Cologne, Dusseldorf, Hamburg, and Munich).

The empirical findings for the creative class (CC) are also very similar to those for the creative sector. This observation can also depend on strong (knowledge) externalities. This result confirms Florida's theoretical assumption that there is a self-reinforcing process on the creative class. One part of this assumption is that the creative class is heavily concentrated on some agglomerated places.

The alternative findings for the third econometric equation (5.3), which suggests that a large initial share of high-skilled agents affects the growth in the share of high-skilled agents (EDU on $\triangle EDU$), suggest that the high-skilled agents expand in the same way as the creative sector or creative class does: The regions with initially scarce educational (human) capital grow faster in high-skilled agents than those regions with initially higher educational (human) capital shares. Whether we observe the coefficient for AGG_EDU (interaction term of EDU with AGG), the assumption of a convergence process turns out to be wrong. There is an indication that potential human capital externalities lead to a further accumulation of high-skilled agents in already highly agglomerated regions.[4]

Research question 3, hypothesis 6. The empirical results further suggest that bohemians are differently distributed between the regions. Agglomerated regions with a relatively high concentration of bohemians affect local employment growth in the creative sector. Under the assumption that creative agents value the level of cultural amenity (approximated by bohemians) while less-creative agents do not, the relative supply of creative agents is unequally distributed between the regions.

This observation can also be found in the "real" world. The observation that creative agents value cultural amenities seems to be realistic, since they are assumed to be more mobile than less-creative agents.[5] In consequence, there is not necessarily an equilibrium in creative professionals belonging to the creative sector between the regions. This observation is consistent with the results for AGG_BOH_{it-3}. The interpretation is that agglomerated regions with high cultural amenities are able to attract employment in general, but also creative agents in particular. Furthermore, those already agglomerated regions pool a certain critical mass of bohemians, which might be of relevance for the production of cultural-related goods.

This result also verify Florida's hypothesis that cultural-related professions have a positive effect on employment growth. Bohemians self generate new products and processes. However, creative professionals are interpreted as being attracted to those places that are most beneficial to creative and innovative activities. [6]

---

4 These results are contradict to Suedekum's (2006; 2008) empirical results on human capital externalties and high-skilled employment growth. He suggests that high- and medium-skilled workers are imperfect substitutes, which would explain why cities with high-initial shares of high-skilled agents will grow more moderately: As a result, the cities will converge to each other. See, for the discussion on local human capital and skill specific employment growth in Germany also, for example, Schlitte (2010).
5 Cf. for the discussion on creative professionals' mobility chapter 2.
6 Moreover, empirical results from Falck et al. (2009) or Wojan et al. (2007), for instance, show similar results. If I compare these results with Möller and Tubadji (2009) or Wedemeier (2010a,b), this view is not empirically supported. This can be mainly explained by differences in the methodology, in definitions, and the regional level of investigation.

6.2. Conclusions

Given the empirical evidence above, it is possible to draw a link to the theoretical assumptions. The third chapter introduced a model that helps to explain regional differences in employment growth through externalities (knowledge spillovers). The argument is that creative professionals pool in and continue to accumulate in specific regions: The regions diverge from each other in creative professionals employment. Knowledge spillovers raise local productivity, which results in higher wages and leverages further the amount of sector employment. The presented empirical research explored this aspect and provides supporting evidence for the logic of the theory. It is concluded that not only does the creative sector have an impact on total employment growth, but also on creative sector employment: There is an indication that externalities within highly agglomerated regions lead to a self-reinforcing process. Agglomerated regions with already high shares of creative professionals grow faster than Germany's mean. This will further increase the number of creative professionals at a few single places. This polarisation, however, takes place only in high employment agglomerated regions. In contrast, regions with lower shares of creative professionals will converge to Germany's mean. The results are significant for the creative sector (agents with technological creative abilities), the creative class (employees with technological and economic creative abilities), and high-skilled agents.

However, it is obvious that the creative sector and the creative class differ in several qualitative aspects from the classical human capital measure. But, the results show the same effects for the high-skilled agents. This is not surprising, since the creative sector and the creative class are simultaneously part of creative (human) capital and of educational (human) capital: Both concepts are part of an emerging "knowledge economy".

Here are the five research questions, with the respective concluding results:

1. How important is the creative sector for employment growth?

   The creative sector has a positive economic impact on Germany's total employment growth.

2. How relevant are the economic effects originating from the diversity (of employment) on employment growth?

   Diversity generally affects the growth rate of total employment. That said, it is important to differentiate between the diversity effects of the creative sector itself and of ethnic-cultural diversity, through both positively affect total employment growth.

3. Is there a self-reinforcing process of pooled creative professionals?

There is a self-reinforcing process of pooled creative professionals. However, this effect depends on the spatial type of observation. In terms of the German mean, there is a tendency for the convergence of unequally distributed creative professionals. When the research focus lies on already highly agglomerated regions, there is a clear trend towards further creative professionals accumulating in those regions.

4. What does the regional distribution of creative professionals look like?

   Creative professionals are mainly located in Germany's agglomerated regions. The creative sector's concentration is also more represented in Southern Germany.

5. (a) Are cities places with a higher share of creative professionals, (b) and what (urban) policy instruments strengthen creative sector employment?

   (a) Cities, or agglomerated regions, have higher shares of creative professionals.

   (b) Some policy suggestions for strengthen the creative sector are:

   - Attracting creative professionals, and in general human capital, through provision of a high local supply of cultural amenities.
   - Diversifying the occupational base of the creative sector in order to raise the probability of knowledge spillovers and knowledge collisions.
   - Increasing local networks for knowledge sharing between the agents of the creative sector.

Further concrete policy instruments are highlighted in the following chapter, which presents a policy case study on Hamburg's creative sector. This approach provides more information on implemented instruments and policy actions. In the policy case study, I also present new data for reasons of topicality. This data is arranged per the definition of Germany's cultural and creative sector, which comes from the German Parliament. Because of this new data on the creative economy, the conclusions made here maybe considered as conditionally transferable to the case study. However, the results of the empirical study have a general novel value for the research on the creative sector. Therefore, the results and conclusion made in the empirical section (part II) of this thesis have a significant impact for the policy case study.

Part III.

Applications and policy perspective

7. Policy lessons from Hamburg

The seventh chapter presents a case study on Hamburg, Germany, and sets theory into working practice. The chapter contributes, *inter alia*, to the research question 5, which asks if cities are places of high creativity. The question is relevant, particularly because in recent years concepts of creativity based on Florida's (2002) ideas have become increasingly important for urban policy and planning. Following the results of section 5.2, it is concluded that agglomerated regions have the highest shares of agents employed in the creative sector, as well as the highest shares of bohemians. This result goes hand in hand with studies showing that the creative sector is mainly concentrated in urban regions (see, for instance, Andersen and Lorenzen 2005; Florida 2002).

The remainder of the seventh chapter is organised as follows. First, a short statistical introduction including some structural characteristics of Germany's three biggest cities (Berlin, Hamburg, and Munich) is presented. Afterwards, some new detailed figures on the creative sector and its submarkets are highlighted. Based on the city comparison, a strategy for the development of cities' creative sector is formulated. The strategy addresses general economic trends of demographic and structural change: In highly developed countries such as Germany industry jobs are decreasing, while at the same time jobs in the tertiary sector increase. As we will see in section 7.2, this effect leads also to more specialisation towards cultural and creative jobs.[1] Therefore an active focus on strategies to strengthen this sector becomes important. Third, analysing the example of Hamburg's current governmental and non-governmental actions related to the cultural and creative sector are presented and commented. Finally, a summary is provided and consequences for the theory and empiricism are briefly discussed.

7.1. Statistical facts on the city of Hamburg

Cities are the ideal starting points to meet the challenges of demographic and structural change towards culturally rich and creative-based societies. However, cities also compete with each other for firms, qualified labour and other input factors. Table 7.1

---

1 Also, the statistical and econometric analysis in chapter 5 comes to the same conclusions.

offers a short overview of some key structural characteristics of Germany's three biggest cities, Hamburg, Berlin, and Munich. The three cities are quite heterogeneous in terms of their economic structures.[2] By population, Hamburg is Germany's second biggest city (1.761.711 inhabitants) after Berlin (3.407.625 inhabitants). Berlin also has the largest stock of labour force (1.604.006). In 2007, the labour force participation rate is notably higher in Hamburg (63.8 percent) and Munich (65.4 percent) than in Berlin (61.2 percent). The largest productivity and GDP (gross domestic product) is found in Munich. Considering the commuting balance, Munich also has the highest number of incoming commuters (280.900 employees), followed by Hamburg. Measuring the travel time per car and airplane to 41 European agglomerated centres, the city of Berlin has the best connectivity, followed by Hamburg.

Table 7.1.: Structural characteristic of Germany's three biggest cities

Year 2007	Hamburg	Berlin	Munich
Population	1.761.711	3.407.625	1.302.376
Labour force	1.089.853	1.604.006	938.170
GDP per capita in Euro	48.6	24.8	55.9
GDP per labour force in Euro	79.0	52.8	78.2
Forecast of population growth (1)	0.7	0.9	1.5
Commuting balance (2)	269.2	89.7	280.9
Unemployment rate	6.7	11.0	4.8
Municipality debts (3)	23.874	27.991	15.106
Land for building price in Euro/m^2	627.6	271.5	1067.3
Accessability (4)	207	198	208

Notes: (1) 2008-2025; (2) per 1.000 employees; (3) per capita in Euro in 2008; (4) of 41 European agglomeration centres in minutes.
Source: Federal Office for Building and Regional Planning (2010), Initiative Neue Soziale Marktwirtschaft (2011), own calculations.

Table 7.2 shows the distribution of the cultural- and creative sector within the three cities, based on current data from the Federal Employment Agency (Bundesagentur für Arbeit [Federal Employment Agency] 2010) and on the economic sector classification of the German parliament (Söndermann 2009; Söndermann et al. 2009; Wirtschaftsminis-terkonferenz 2009).[3] Among the three cities, in 2008 Hamburg again had the second

---

2 For the transition of Hamburg's economy, see, for example, Boje et al. (2010).

3 In this section, I use the definition of the cultural and creative sector coming from the German parliament. The difference with the concept used previously is that the definition used here focuses mainly on culturally related professions. From the creative sector only the creative submarkets advertisement, software and the games industry as well as publishing are included. Furthermore, the definition of the cultural and creative sector is based on a industrial classification, and vice versa the former definition of the agents working in creative professions is based on an occupational classification. As a result, the definition from the German parliament overestimates the employment effect coming from the creative

highest share of cultural and creative sector employment in relation to total employment (6.9 percent). In contrast, Munich had 8.1 and Berlin 5.8 percent of the overall employment located in the cultural and creative sector.[4] In absolute numbers, however, Berlin is ranked first, followed by Hamburg. In general, the software and games submarket has the biggest share of employees within the cultural and creative sector, followed by the advertisement submarket. In 2008, Hamburg had one of the highest shares in Germany in both submarkets (software and games 23.7 percent, advertisement 20.3 percent), while with 11.219 employees, publishing is the third biggest submarket of Hamburg's cultural and creative sector.[5] Berlin is ranked first in the submarket cultural activities. Hamburg's cultural and creative sector increased its share of employment by 5.3 percent, Berlin by 13 percent, and Munich by 17.1 percent.[6]

Table 7.3 shows the growth in eleven submarkets between 2003 and 2008. Software and games had one of the highest growth rates for all three cities. Considerable differences between the cities can particularly be found in the publishing submarket, in which employment decreased in Hamburg (-21.7 percent) and increased in Berlin (13.1 percent) as well as in Munich (4.8 percent).[7]

To sum up, these short statistical findings highlight that these cities all face similar global challenges, while the policy implications for the creative sector should (eminently) differ between the three cities. Second, looking at the labour force participation rate, and also at unemployment, it seems that Hamburg and Munich have a more efficient allocation

---

professions self. However, since the case study shall provide governance actions to policy makers, a clear cut definition seems not to be highly relevant. More important is the relative up-to-date applicability, which is essential for policy making. Furthermore, at this point it is not the research focus to present a detailed statistical overview on Hamburg's cultural and creative sector.

4 Recall that using the IAB-Regionalfile 1975-2004 data, in 1975 and 2004 Hamburg had a relatively high share of agents with technological creative ability (6.8 and 10.5 percent). Altogether, the shares of agents with technological and cultural creative ability was 8.2 and 12.4 percent in 1975 and 2004. In comparison, Munich had the highest shares in Germany of technological employees both in year 1975 and 2004 (10.5 and 15.7 percent). The share of bohemians was 1.3 (year 1975) and 2.0 percent (year 2004).

5 In appendix A.1.12, the data for year 2003 are provided.

6 In Hamburg, the service sector increased its share of the labour market between 2003 and 2008 (8.9 percent), while the industrial sector decreased by -3.0 percent. Generally, significant structural differences in the transition cannot be found between the three cities. For more details on the structural change of the city of Hamburg, see, for instance Boje et al. (2010).

7 Hamburg lost relatively high numbers of creative sector employees, especially agents working in the field of publishing and music. Many of them moved to the capital city Berlin. For instance, two big companies partially moved, with their employees, from Hamburg to Berlin, Axel Springer multimedia company and Universal Music. However, many independent and individual artists also moved to Berlin after the fall of the Berlin wall. There are different reasons for this development. In this transition, many agents migrated to Berlin, since Germany's capital city was more attractive to individual agents with creative ability and cheaper housing (see, for example, Frank and Mundelius 2005; Mundelius 2009): Berlin's city structure was, and is, more unorthodox than that of other German cities and therefore more attractive to creative professionals.

with their labour forces than Berlin. Third, the municipalities debts are heterogeneously distributed. Both Berlin and Hamburg have some of the highest municipal debt rates in Germany. Munich, on the other hand, is one of the best performing German cities, at least in terms of municipal debt. These findings provide different scopes for policy action. Research question 5 (b) asks what (urban) strategies and instruments cities can use to influence the development of the creative sector. Although Florida's insights received strong criticism, his perspectives and political suggestions have been implemented by many local and regional authorities.[8,9] This work now turns its focal point to examples of policy actions in the city of Hamburg.

Table 7.2.: Cultural and creative sector employment (2008)

	Hamburg total	share of		Berlin total	share of		Munich total	share of	
Submarket (1)	(2)	(3)		(2)	(3)		(2)	(3)	
Publishing	11,219	17.0	1.2	8,797	11.8	0.7	12,093	18.2	1.5
Motion pictures	3,617	5.5	0.4	8,375	11.2	0.7	4,052	6.1	0.5
Radio/television	5,415	8.2	0.6	4,550	6.1	0.4	5,722	8.6	0.7
Cultural activities	6,422	9.7	0.7	9,635	12.9	0.8	5,158	7.8	0.6
Journalist	1,320	2.0	0.1	1,515	2.0	0.1	747	1.1	0.1
Library/museums	1,939	2.9	0.2	4,088	5.5	0.3	1,768	2.7	0.2
Trade with cultural goods	2,717	4.1	0.3	3,316	4.4	0.3	2,320	3.5	0.3
Architecture	3,299	5.0	0.3	5,321	7.1	0.4	3,090	4.7	0.4
Design (4)	11,102	16.8	1.2	7,723	10.4	0.6	9,339	14.1	1.1
Advertising (4)	13,377	20.3	1.4	10,447	14.0	0.8	11,206	16.9	1.4
Software/Games	15,656	23.7	1.6	17,872	24.0	1.4	19,356	29.2	2.4
Cultural/ creative sector (5)	65,985	100	6.9	74,589	100	5.8	66,395	100	8.1

Notes: Employees who are subject to compulsory insurance deductions, ; (1) Wirtschaft-szweigklassifikation (WZ) 2008, WZ-Number 3 and 5. see also A.1.11 in the appendix; (2) creative economy; (3) overall economy; (4) with double count; (5) without double count. Source: Bundesagentur für Arbeit [Federal Employment Agency] (2010), definition based on Söndermann (2009); Wirtschaftsministerkonferenz (2009), own calculations.

---

8 For a synopsis of the criticism see chapter 2.3.
9 There is already a relatively large number of literature on the potential of the cultural and creative sector for German cities as Berlin (see, for example, Besecke et al. 2008: Evans and Witting 2006; Frank and Mundelius 2005: Hesse and Lange 2007; Mundelius 2009) and Munich (see, for example, Hafner et al. 2007).

Table 7.3.: Growth of the cultural and creative sector employment (2003-08)

Submarket (1)	Hamburg Growth 2003-2008 (2)	Berlin	Munich
Publishing	-21.7	13.1	4.8
Motion pictures and video	9.4	13.9	-0.9
Radio and television	-15.6	-9.3	15.2
Cultural activities	21.2	2.7	13.8
Journalist and newcast	10.6	0.7	28.1
Library and museums	4.8	1.9	-21.2
Trade with cultural goods	5.8	22.2	-23.6
Architecture	14.4	3.5	-7.9
Design (3)	21.3	32.1	54.0
Advertisement (3)	7.2	24.1	56.5
Software and Games	24.6	23.4	25.6
Cultural and creative sector (4)	5.3	13.0	17.1

Notes: Employees who are subject to compulsory insurance deductions. (1) Wirtschaft-szweigklassifikation (WZ) 2008. WZ-Number 3 and 5, see also A.1.11 in the appendix; (2) Growth is calculated by $growth_t = ln(variable_t) - ln(variable_{t-1})$; (3) with double count; (4) without double count.
Source: Bundesagentur für Arbeit [Federal Employment Agency] (2010). definition based on Söndermann (2009); Wirtschaftsministerkonferenz (2009). own calculations.

7.2. Strategies and policy actions

Giving the ongoing structural change. the demand for (high-)skilled labour is to continue expanding. The current tendency within this structural change has been the growth of demand for high-skilled labour in the service sector. but the cultural and creative sectors will further experience growth in Hamburg. One crucial point in this discussion. however. are agglomeration effects that encourage the upcoming service sector: In agglomerations. face-to-face contacts facilitate spillovers of (new) knowledge. especially in branches such as design. architecture. or research and development. Through the fact that cities have less physical space between individual agents. firms. or (formal) institutions. face-to-face contacts might occur more often in cities. Since there is also an enormous change in the product range as well as in approaches and ways of working. new businesses and services will further increase. Generally. there are more jobs on offer in cities. but companies in cities also face scarce human resources. as they increasingly seek special skills. education. and capabilities. Firms take this scarcity into account in their decision on location. after all companies follow people (see. for instance. Geppert and Gornig 2010; Florida 2005;

Fritsch and Stützer 2006).[10] This scarcity is also caused and intensified by demographic change. Countries like Germany have high and fast growing shares of elderly people. Yet, this demographic change differs between cities and rural regions: In German cities, the population increased between 1998 and 2008, while Germany's total population decreased in the same period (see Geppert and Gornig 2010). The process of a shrinking population contributes to the increasing importance of cities, since the critical mass of agents for specific working processes is located in cities rather than in rural regions. In the end, Hamburg does not only compete for (high-)skilled labour, and in consequence for companies, with other German cities, but also with other European and international cities.

Therefore, cities such as Hamburg increasingly have to strengthen their local attractiveness in order to attract agents, but also to keep people in place. In a globalised economy, cities - especially high-wage cities - have to draw their comparative advantage from creative and knowledge products, and economic agents are their "ingredients". (High-)skill and relatively labour-intensive tasks - as those in creative professions generally are - are mainly located in cities (see Storper and Scott 2009, or Chapter 5 of this book). The division of labour and specialisation within firms and between sectors improves productivity, but the division of labour is limited by the extent of products, markets, and embodied knowledge (i.e. tacit knowledge): "the more knowledge is tacit, the more difficult it is to share it between people, firms and regions" (Lundvall 1996, 6). An advantage of cities with relatively high shares of high-skilled and creative agents is that embodied knowledge can be properly allocated and organised between the firms and individual agents. In contrast, routinised and capital-intensive operations like industrial production tend to be located in smaller cities or rural areas (see Storper and Scott 2009; Storper and Venables 2004). Generally, in order to strengthen their local competitiveness cities should develop strategies based on detailed analyses of their status quo and perspectives. Cities should ask several questions to deal with, for instance, what sorts of activities and actions - cultural, economic, or housing - should be employed to achieve wealthy urban regions? What kind of branding is necessary so that a specific city is known in the world? How can a city attract and address economic agents? What are the strengths, weaknesses, opportunities, and threats for the city ? Or what are potential clusters (see Hospers 2003)?

In a formulated strategy various soft location factors, such as cultural amenities, are seen as being elementary to further development. The competitiveness and cultural amenities of cities have gained a more and more important position in urban planning. Both go hand in hand: the latter being a means for the former. This presupposes a suitable

---

10 This discussion is controversially debated, since agents' individual choices can also be redirected through preference-seeking, i.e. people follow jobs as well (see, *inter alia*, (Storper and Scott 2009).

environment, in which it is possible to implement new ideas, and in which agents ability can prosper. This requires both openness and the courage to move away from outdated thought patterns and behaviour. These qualities in turn depend to a high degree on soft locational factors. A benefit for cities can be to develop special characteristics and instruments to hold, to attract and to advance creative agents. Cities such as London (United Kingdom) or Toronto (Canada), but also small- and medium-sized cities like Aarhus (Denmark) or Graz (Austria) have already integrated the strategy of being creative city into their urban planning (see, for instance, Evans 2006; Freeman 2008; Gertler et al. 2006; Könönen et al. 2008; Traxler et al. 2006).

The Free and Hanseatic City of Hamburg followed these developments on the creative city, implementing their own integrated approach - formulated in a mission statement - in 2009. The mission statement, "Vision Hamburg: Responsible growth" (*Leitbild Hamburg: Wachsen mit Weitsicht*), focuses on different clusters, among others on maritime economics, life sciences, and the creative sector. Hamburg's goal is to improve these clusters and the creative potential of individual agents in all living areas in order to develop a place, that is more attractive than others. This represents Hamburg's competing for creative agents, but also generally for economic agents. This strategy is not new, but the mission statement also explicitly addresses the creative economy.

Against the background of the results presented in sections 7.1 and 7.2, Hamburg has to further develop their competitiveness in order to ensure welfare and to keep step with the city's competitors. One important step towards tackling the above outlined trends is to strengthen the attractiveness of a city for creative agents. In following, I present some governance techniques that could promote the creative sector. I differentiate between three governance actions, hierarchical governance (top-down), co-governance (public-private partnership), and self-governance (bottom-up).

7.3. Governance actions

Hierarchical- and co-governance. Hamburg's Senate developed different strategies for improving local conditions relevant to the creative economy and its stakeholders. Since 2008, the Senate of Hamburg has put forward a mission statement, which among other things focuses on the development of the creative sector (Mitteilung des Senats an die Bürgerschaft 2009, 2010). One political strategy of the Hamburg senate is to strengthen the "creative economy" cluster, which is meant to give impulse to the further development of this cluster. The above econometric results show that higher local shares of the creative sector reinforce the economic effect coming from creative professionals already located in the area. This proximity effect may reinforce the spillover effect of knowledge through face-to-face contacts among the agents, i.e. a positive externality. Moreover, proximity may provide the diffusion process of embodied, that is the diffusion of tacit, and specialised knowledge: Clustering helps to link the heavily specialised economic agents; it may help to bridge the gap between the Smithian division of labour. The econometric results of the work at hand, furthermore, show that cluster strategies should be adopted, since the pooling of creative agents matters for employment growth. One of the most important and novel aspect of the results analysis, however, is that the structure of the pooled creative sector itself should be diverse.

Studies have shown that clustering in the creative sector is different from conventional clusters, since creative sector clusters not only have economic, but also social objectives such as the inclusion of all different agent groups (see Baycan-Levent 2010). These socio-economic differences are visible in the mission statement of the city of Hamburg. The city tries to address different aspects of the creative sector, for example, through the creation of better conditions for the Hamburg Welcome Center,[11] through the identification and development of new instruments to strengthen creative urban quarters, by attempting to attract creative agents in neighbouring countries and in other parts of Germany itself, and through boosting the cultural scene (movie, music, and theatre).

With these economic and urban policy aspects, the Senate developed tools, which shall help to strengthen Hamburg's creative and innovative potentials. The mission statement is also connected to different Senate projects such as "Creative Hamburg" (*Kreatives Hamburg*), and "Hamburg: home port" (*Hamburg: Heimathafen*), which have explicit policy plans. For example, within the "Creative Hamburg" program, the local government founded the so-called creative agency (*Kreativ Gesellschaft mbH*) in 2009, which shall, for instance, support Hamburg's creative entrepreneurs on the local real estate market.[12] The motivation for this policy intervention is the relatively scarcity of cheap real estate in Hamburg, but cultural and creative entrepreneurs are considered to generate low-incomes, which is a potential conflict (see, for example, Besecke et al. 2008; Mundelius 2009). Other activities initiated by the creative agency are the organisation of network conferences such as "11bar" for cultural and creative entrepreneurs, which is an organised conference, but with user-generated content and an open character (so-called BarCamps conferences). Within the action "Hamburg: home port" the Senate recognised

---

11 For instance, the Hamburg Welcome Center provides service mainly to new citizens from abroad, but also to citizens coming from within Germany. The centre helps new citizens to manage legal aspects of their life, such as registration for income tax or authorisation of residence.

12 One of the newest real estate projects of the creative agency is that of the urban quarter *Oberhafen HafenCity*. Together with the HafenCity Hamburg GmbH (a full company of the city of Hamburg) they develop a strategy for the transformation of the former Oberhafen logistics area into an urban quarter for creative professionals.

the idea of agents' diversity for city development. The working assumption is that the ethnic-cultural diversity encourages places with a creative, open environment (see Florida 2002, 2005; Pohl 2008). However, more important is the contribution of ethnic-cultural diversity to different local knowledge bases. On the other side, a necessary strategy is also to incorporate active integrating employment policies for those agents with migration backgrounds. Here, Hamburg's government embedded a strategy for, e.g., housing, and for integration in a wider social process, which is essential since trust relations between the different individual agents for co-operative actions and employment are needed. Within this strategy, it is possible to address single urban neighbourhoods with different socio-economic development patterns.[13]

Local and institutional knowledge should also be connected to external linkages, for instance, through cross-border interactions between cities. This practice brings new ideas to urban development and is the best way to break through crusted institutional, social, and cultural settings (see, for instance, Maskell et al. 1998). New knowledge can lead to a wide range of inventions, which can result in innovative products (see, for instance, Hospers 2003; Schumpeter 1950). Via cross-border interactions cities are able to connect local and institutional knowledge and to address agents from different cities and regions. In this context, in March 2010 the city of Hamburg set up an agreement on the interregional exchange of cultural as well as creative entrepreneurship with the Øresund Region.[14] This policy action can be helpful, since the Øresund Region with its small economies is known as an experimental city region for new technologies and cultural products.[15] Another policy would be to implement active twinning agreements between cities.

More than that, the Hamburg Marketing Company - a company of the city of Hamburg - tries to address and to attract agents and companies. The marketing company produces a lifestyle magazine about Hamburg (title: "Hamburg: The Magazine from the Metropolis"), which is distributed as a supplement in several nationwide daily newspapers in Germany and Austria. Within the magazine, but also through other channels, the city of Hamburg presents itself as a brand and tries to underline its unique character with this strategy. In the increasing competition between cities, there is a major role for marketing to play. Both interregional exchange and branding actions can bring further stimulus to urban evolution: It can attract individual agents and single firms.

---

13 Pohl shows in a study of the distribution of the creative sector in Hamburg "that a high rate of openness to diversity does not [necessarily] entail improvements in socio-spatial development" Pohl (2008, 317).
14 The Øresund Region consists of Southern Sweden (Malmö and Lund) and Eastern Denmark (Greater Copenhagen area). Approximately 3.6 million inhabitants live in this region.
15 Several studies show the relevance of test and experimental markets, and the Scandinavian countries particularly function as such markets (see, for example, Maskell et al. 1998).

Successful transformations require governmental and non-governmental institutions that can drive ideas forward through individual dedications. Governmental initiatives - for example the "international building exhibition (IBA) Hamburg" (Internationale Bauausstellung (IBA) Hamburg) - bundles governmental and non-governmental actions. The IBA Hamburg - another independent company owned by the city of Hamburg - has different key themes, which shall forward IBA Hamburg's mission of developing solutions for the future of urbanity and community. The exhibition has an experimental character, which tests tools as active public participation on specific urban problems, for example gentrification and segregation. New lifestyles and new cultures come up against each other, and at that borderline the IBA Hamburg tries to put forward platforms, products and attitudes for urban life to bring the different groups and people together. These changes also lead to new products and businesses. Today, cities such as Hamburg are marked by the ethnic-cultural diversity, but the individuals live mostly separated in homogenised neighbourhoods and urban quarters (see, for example, Storper and Scott 2009, or Pohl 2008). For Hamburg this is partially true, since individuals are also segregated by income (see, for instance, Pohl 2008). IBA Hamburg's mission is, however, to bring social inclusion into neighbourhoods with high shares of migrants and to minimise risks of social disorder through strategies such as the "uses of pavements" see Jacobs 1992. The idea is that inhabitants, firms and creative professionals can meet on cultural or social platforms for discussions and co-operative actions. The exhibition functions in this context as a moderator and works to foster trusting relationships among the different groups and individuals. Important is the competence of IBA Hamburg to create space and opportunities for the communication between the individual agents (see Klotz and Theis 2010). However, the socio-spatial diversion of urban quarters is not directly encountered as part of this strategy, since IBA is fixed on the low-income urban quarters Wilhelmsburg, Veddel, and Harburg Harbour.

Results on the location of the creative quarters by Overmeyer et al. (2010) further suggests cities reinforce and strengthen urban characteristics by using planning tools that encourage mixed urban areas and the accentuation of authentic neighbourhood characters. The argument is that creative professionals prefer to live in such unique neighbourhoods, since cultural and creative products are results of unorthodox ideas and skills: The neighbourhoods give the impulses for novel products. Criticism arises however, if urban quarters are facing gentrification, i.e. when wealthy agents begin buying up or renting housing in less wealthy quarters. The criticism of this is that it changes the unique character of quarters and communities. Gentrification is, *vice versa*, also a strategy to create a more mixed-use urban quarter, though it can cause the crowding out of less wealthy agents to the suburban areas, which results in segregation and polarisation. It is an area of conflict, a phenomenon known as the "self-destruction of [urban] diversity" (Jacobs 1992, 241). In this context, Florida (2009) suggests that government policies should encourage renting and not house ownership. The idea is that renting is much more flexible and can faster react to market supply and demand changes. Florida's argument is that house ownership makes the agents too dependent on one single place, but an economy, in order to react to shocks, requires the presence of non-anchored agents. In this context, the accumulation of creative professionals is linked to a higher turnover and circulation of economic agents within a city. This also goes along with negative externalities, for instance, with regard to family structures, gentrification, or housing prices (see, for example, Sassen 2001). All these aspects must be taken into consideration when it comes to the urban planning of neighbourhoods in the context of creative professionals, but also in general in the context of urban socio-economic policies.

Besides the governmental instruments of the Hamburg Senate, the chamber of commerce has its own focus on the creative sector,[16] and in Hamburg the Federal Ministry of Economics and Technology has a regional competency centre, which give advice to companies in the creative sector.

Self-governance. Non-governmental initiatives like the privately initiated *Kultur-Palast Hamburg* with its Hip Hop Academy (music), the media and information technology network Hamburg@work with its sections Gamecity, Linux, and Crossmedia, or the internationally known self-governing *Reeperbahn Festival* (music and arts) can have a vital influence on the development of Hamburg's creative sector.

An open, mutually attitude between governmental and non-governmental stakeholders is important, because it facilitate the unified discussion of possible development plans. After all, face-to-face contacts are a locational advantage of cities. The concept of face-to-face and know-who, i.e. who knows what to do and who knows how (Lundvall 1996), is important to building successful networks among economic agents.[17] Networks force agents to define strategic interactions and push intensive, comprehensive co-operations (for the discussion on networks and co-operation, see, for example, Elsner 2000). An example of a strategic network of firms is the "Hamburg music community (IHM)" (*Interessengemeinschaft Hamburger Musikwirtschaft*, IHM). Within the IHM, various small, medium, and large-scale enterprises from the music are interlinked, such as music publishers, music labels, concert organisers, or innkeepers. The IHM is a network that develops and intensifies long-lasting co-operations within the music scene, with the aim of improving its

---

16 The chamber of trade is a self-regulatory organisation with some degree of common law and regulatory authority.
17 In return, these concepts also plays a crucial role within small- and medium-sized cities, since they help to bundle and arrange expertise.

competitiveness. The network helps to develop trust relationships between the different economic agents. Trust is especially relevant in the field of creative and experience-based sectors as music or media are (see Florida et al. 2010; Maskell and Lorenzen 2004b). In this context innovations are the result of "collective entrepreneurship", the result of interactive co-operations. In consequence, trust cannot be imposed by local authorities; trust relations have to be developed and to grow evolutionary, from below.

The relative strength of Hamburg's cultural amenities, the relative diversity of economic agents and the relative size of the creative sector suggest a base on which to build (see also Gertler et al. 2002). This suggests that the different levels of government that affect innovation, art, immigration or settlement should create the conditions for the creative sector in the context of urban economic development. The threat is that possible political actions become standardise and reduce agents' creative abilities, since their abilities reflect a criticism of the existing state of politics and products. Therefore, strong non-governmental initiatives are especially needed, since the creative sector is an unorthodox sector, which cluster its economic agents with different social and economical backgrounds.

7.4. Interim summary and conclusions

Summary. This chapter has presented some current statistics on demography, income, and creative activities in the city of Hamburg. Policy examples for the promotion of Hamburg's creative sector were then discussed, and the impressions from Hamburg demonstrate how governmental and non-governmental actions can improve the conditions for individual economic agents and companies. It is suggested that network strategies foster the interactions between agents, policy makers and social stakeholders. This is a precondition for the exchange of knowledge and ideas. The empirical analysis points in the same direction. Just as important are the communication skills and will to communicate between responsible stakeholders for urban development. In particular for economic development, co-operation is the main achievement in forming clusters and reducing disadvantages of scale (cf. Könönen et al. 2008). Local initiatives like the strategic firm network of Hamburg's music community (IHM) show how private actions improve the local network and competitive conditions. The examples generally illustrate, however, that local governments cannot draw blue prints for creativity and innovation. In the course of coming progressive demographic change, the example of Hamburg shows that it is no longer sufficient to demonstrate excellence as an educational or creative location within national borders. As internationality increases, the focus needs to lie also on the recruitment of firms, (creative) professionals, inhabitants, and labour from abroad. Therefore, an action focus is to formulate and introduce a clear city branding as a strategy.[18] This branding strategy should determine the unique local character in which a city like Hamburg can distinguish itself from other cities, and not as a city is known for being a "knowledge and university city" like all others.

Conclusions. The example from Hamburg presents strategies for clustering and networking. The empirical results of chapter 5 indicate that the regional concentration of the creative sector matters for total employment growth, and also that the diversity of the group of creative professionals itself matters. Moreover, the empirical analysis indicates that agglomerated regions with high shares of creative agents are subject to self-reinforcing processes. High housing prices and other congestion costs may possibly distort this process. Furthermore, as discussed in the review, theory, and empirical chapters, it is strategically important to allocate all individual agents - including those with migration in their background - and incorporate them into the labour market and productivity. Ultimately, the needed focus on action depends on a city's level of economic development. The development must be ascertained by analyses and reflected upon objectively by various stakeholders. Urban and regional development depends on evolutionary processes that are socially, economically, and historically path dependent, thence there is no policy instrument which allows a "one-size-fits-all" approach. However, the policy oriented case study needs to be reflected in the context of a further empirical application. With a further-going (theoretical, analytical, and) empirical contribution, the results may be more stringent (and robust) than deterministic.

---

18 Thierstein and Goebel (2007) discuss in this context the use of maritime pictures in the city branding of Hamburg. They conclude that the use of maritime pictures is overused. Moreover, the sectoral shift towards the knowledge economy should be more accentuated in the marketing strategy of the city of Hamburg.

Part IV.

A final overview

8. Conclusions

In this thesis the impact of the creative sector on employment growth in German regions from 1977 to 2004 is investigated. This sector was highly dynamic in the last decades and is currently much debated in economic research. It is furthermore one of the recent important topics in regional and city planning. However, the work has been specifically concerned with the creative sector's impact on total employment growth and group specific employment growth, i.e. the growth of employment in the creative sector. The assumption is that employment pooling in the creative sector might result in the further accumulation of employment in the creative sector. This assumption proves to be a self-reinforcing process.

Before the empirical investigation into this research question, I introduced and developed a model of the creative city based on Suedekum (2006, 2008). This model was to explain the above employment effect on the creative sector, including the circular effect of cultural amenities (i.e. centripetal forces). This model of the creative city helps to interpret the direction and logic of the empirical results. However, the main result of this research is the following: I find robust evidence for the positive influence of the creative sector that fosters the regional growth rate of total employment. The presence of large shares of creative professionals lead to an increase in total employment, but reduce the growth rate of the same employment group. The growth in total employment overwhelms the decline of the growth rate of creative professionals. The growth rate is unequally distributed between the regions, since there is a divergence between peripheral and highly agglomerated regions. The results show that an initially large share of regional creative professionals push the regional concentration of those professions forward in agglomerated regions. A further result of this research is that diversity (i.e. creative professionals and ethnic-cultural diversity) matters on employment growth, the argument is that it raises the potential of knowledge spillovers.

The rest of this chapter is organised as follows. Section 8.1 presents the summary of the main findings. This section is organised into descriptions of the conceptual background and theory (part I), the empirical work (part II), and the policy impact given in the thesis. The last part of the section summarises applications and policy perspectives from

Hamburg, Germany (part III). Section 8.2 discusses the works limitations and presents possible future research topics and, finally, the work closes with a final remark.

8.1. Summary of findings

Conceptual background and theory.   The creative sector is regarded as one of the driving forces of employment growth. Florida (2002) - who is heavily influenced by the economics of human capital - has been the main proponent of this idea of the creative sector. His simple but pioneering idea was to measure human capital by professions: The creative professionals. These economic agents - working in the field of education, engineering, science, and arts - form the creative sector. Florida additionally applied Jacobs' (1969) concept of urban neighbourhoods and economic diversity to explain the location decisions of those creative professionals. Both concepts are an integrated part of the creative city, which is a city that is economically driven by the creative sector.

The creative sector is supposed to play an important role in innovation processes. It is argued that agents working in this sector raise the number of varieties of entrepreneurial activities, or in other words, that they transform ideas and inventions into novel businesses. According to Florida (2002; 2003; 2004; 2005) the economic diversity contributes to creative cities' economic growth and competitiveness due to its positive impact on knowledge and human capital. Regarding the aspect of diversity, the overall arguments in the reviewed literature are that diversity brings variance to knowledge bases, experiences, and (knowledge) networks into work processes. Both the creative sector and diversity are assumed to be indicators capturing the "creative capacity" of cities and regions (Gülümser et al. 2010; Wedemeier 2010b). Of course, the concept of the creative sector is hard to operationalise and with its weak and fuzzy theoretical model, nonetheless, this sectoral approach has an increasingly large influence on research studying innovation, and economic and employment growth. Florida's "perspectives has been readily qualified via the implementation of new creativity based political actions initiated by local and regional authorities" (Pohl 2008, 317). However, a main criticism is raised by Glaeser (2005), who condemns Florida (2002) for his arguments that the effect coming from the creative (human) capital is stronger than the effect coming from educational (human) capital itself. Running some econometric estimations, Glaeser (2005) concludes that human capital is more relevant for growth than creative (human) capital. Marrocu and Paci (2010) confirm this result. In contrast, using structural equation models and path analysis Florida et al. (2008) find that human capital (educational measure) and the creative sector (occupational measure) affect regional development in different ways. Human capital outperforms in affecting regional income. The creative sector performs better in accounting for regional labour productivity. However, theoretical research about the interrelation of employment growth, creative sector employment growth and the creative sector is astonishingly underdeveloped, given the topicality of the debate.

Novel in this controversy over the creative sector, I introduce two models explaining the relevance of the creative sector on employment growth. First, the theory in chapter 3 provides theoretical arguments that in their essence rely on Murphy et al. (1991). This model supports Florida's view that some agents contribute more to creativity and production than others. The model presents the idea that the most able creative agent switches between both the rent creating and rent seeking sector, depending on the institutional setting and rent opportunities. Whether an economic agent is active in the rent creating sector, depends therefore on the agent's creative ability and on the opportunity to seek rents. Since the model does not explain growth differences within countries - it explains growth differences between countries - only the central arguments are presented. The model helps to explain why creative agents contribute more to economic growth than other agents.

Second, and more importantly, I formulate a model built on Suedekum (2006, 2008). This model is that of the creative city. It is suggested that in the long run there is a stable equilibrium of a constant number of creative agents between two cities if human capital externalities do not exists ($\gamma = 0$), meaning the exchange of ideas and knowledge occurs *inter alia* through face-to-face contacts. On the other hand, employment growth positively depends on the initial share of creative agents if strong externalities exists ($\gamma > 0$). In the case that employment growth is negatively correlated with the initial share of creative agents, it might turn out that the externalities are not strong enough. This does not, however, automatically mean that low externalities have a negative effect on the rate of growth. In conclusion, the model by Suedekum (2006, 2008) helps to specify the econometric model and, more important, to explain the empirical results made in the third part of this thesis.

Germany's creative sector and its impact on employment growth: Empirical analysis. Chapter 5 investigated whether there is an employment effect streaming from the creative sector. The empirical section further aimed to study whether the empirical evidence is consistent with Florida's assumption of a self-reinforcing process: High shares of creative professionals may lead to higher growth rates of the same employment group. The econometric model is built on Suedekum's (2006, 2008) theoretical model, however, the aim of the empirical analysis is not to quantify the size of potential externalities. Using fixed effect models, I present novel results for two different creative sector approaches:

The creative sector and Florida's creative class. Furthermore, an education based approach has been tested. The results differ eminently in space, depending on whether the effect is observed for agglomerated or more peripheral regions, but not between the three definitions.

The implications and conclusions from the empirical estimations are as follows. I find empirical evidence supporting the logic of the theory. A novel result in the empirical research on the creative sector is the conclusion that there is an indication for externalities, since a self-reinforcing process for agglomerated regions with already high shares of creative professionals is observed. The results are significant for the creative sector (agents with technological and cultural creative abilities), the creative class (agents with technological, cultural, and economic creative abilities), and high-skilled agents. I find robust evidence that the creative sector fosters the regional growth rate of total employment. Large shares of creative professionals lead to an increase in total employment, but reduce the growth of the same employment group. Ultimately, the growth in total employment overwhelms the decline of the growth rate of creative professionals. On the other hand, the growth rate is unequally distributed between the regions. A divergence between peripheral and highly agglomerated regions is visible. The results show that an initially large share of regional creative professionals pushes further the regional concentration of those professions in highly agglomerated regions.

Driving forces for the concentration are unobservable city specific characteristics such as regional knowledge spillovers. The result suggests that creative sector pooling benefits particularly from knowledge sharing, and this sector might require as well a specialised knowledge concentration. Other observable characteristics are further identified as a driving force for this concentration, such as local (cultural) amenities (measured by the share of bohemians). These results are additionally confirmed for high-skilled agents. It is obvious that the creative sector and the creative class differ in several qualitative aspects from the classical human capital definition. Nonetheless, both the creative sector and the creative class are simultaneously part of creative (human) capital and educational (human) capital.

One further interesting result is that the local concentration of bohemians positively affects the total and sector specific employment growth. High shares of bohemians attract further employment. These findings are also apparent for creative sector diversity and ethnic-cultural diversity. Both are regarded as locational factors as well, but more importantly, they are regarded as a factor for the creation and distribution of new knowledge. This might further push the regional spillover of knowledge.

Applications and policy perspective. Apart from the theory and empirical chapters, I presented a case study on the creative sector of the city of Hamburg. Policy actions are discussed to show, how special urban problems linked to the creative city are addressed by Hamburg's politicians and social stakeholders. One result of this case study is its making clear that policy agents should pay attention to creative professionals and ethnic-cultural diversity. The argument is that an atmosphere of openness increases the competitiveness in terms of attracting skilled economic agents and diversifying the knowledge basis. Consequently, urban policies should be aware of the importance of soft location factors and urban space for (diverse) communities. Since soft location factors are affected by various fields of policy an intersectoral approach is needed. Parallel actions in major fields of urban policy do not address problems of modernity. Economic, financial, migration, educational, innovation, firm and business policy within cities must be merged into interdependent actions. An integrated approach also pools expertise and financial resources. Furthermore, the concepts of face-to-face and know-who (i.e. who knows what to do and who knows how) accelerates the diffusion of knowledge. Networks among cities play a crucial role, especially for smaller cities since they bundle expertise and financial activities as well. In its institutional dimension, networks stabilise trust relations, co-operation, and networks reduce transaction costs. Policy and economic agents should therefore facilitate co-operative actions. A further approach to avoid petrified structures is to create a reform oriented climate within cities. When a diverse labour pool exists in cities, it might facilitate the diffusion of knowledge as a positive external effect on creativity, innovation and localised growth. However, knowledge sharing depends *inter alia* on the constitution of the labour market and on (formal and informal) institutions. Beside network strategies, policy should focus on cluster strategies to reinforce the pooling of creative professsionals and local knowledge.

8.2. Future research and a final remark

Future research. It is often the case in scientific research that more questions than answers are produced. In this respect, my research is no different from other work. A first limitation of this thesis is that its empirical work is based on relatively old data (1977 to 2004). One research improvement would be by using the newest and newly revised version of the IAB. This new data, SIAB (Sample of Integrated Labour Market Biographies), is available as a scientific usefile from end 2011, and it includes observations up to 2008. Nevertheless, the empirical section contains novel results concerning the creative sector and its effect on total and sector specific employment growth. The time period also covers 27 years, which is a remarkably long time period.

Beside data and methodological aspects - such as using different instrumental variables or beta-coefficients to measure the relative importance of the variables outcome - future investigations may start by using multiple-indicators multiple-causes (MIMIC) and dynamic multiple-indicators multiple-causes (DYMIMIC) models. With these models, the unknown coefficient - the hard to define variable of creativity, i.e. the ability to generate novel knowledge and to utilise present knowledge - are estimated in a set of structural equations. Clearly, these models make it possible to link the unobserved variable to observed indicators. In the case of research on the creative sector, the unobserved variable could be creativity. The assumption is that the variable creativity is linked to and influenced by a set of indicators for creativity. Since there is a large body of literature on the possible causes (for example, creative professionals and agents' diversity) and indicators (for example, patents and income) of creativity, this approach proposes an interesting solution.

Second, following the presentation of this work at conference and seminar discussions, one of the most interesting potential points for future research could be to focus on all occupations in detail. First research steps toward this question have been taken by Gabe and Abel (2011) and Oesch and Menes (2010). With this approach, it is possible to provide answers on questions such as: How is the development of handcraft workers, IT specialists, or performing artists in time? Is there any relationship in time? This research focus can give policy makers and urban developers an answer to the question of who the "right" agent to attract is, how agents can be attracted, and who the "right" companies are. The shift towards the growing influence of the creative sector is a result of industrial restructuring; it is the shift from one specific job to another one. The financial crash of 2008, for instance, destroyed many jobs in the US and worldwide. Yet the economic shock also transformed the economic landscape, possibly towards a more idea-driven, partially employment intensive, creative economy, as Florida (2009) describes. This transition and what it will result in is another fundamental question that scholars and researchers need to discuss.

Third, beside the lack of definition, the relationships between creative sector and export, economic (input-output) linkages, or economic growth are still largely under-researched. In research, the main focus lies just on size and structure of the creative sector (Ye and Yin 2007). For the United Kingdom, Ye and Yin (2007) investigate the economic linkages of the UK creative sector by using input-output tables. The authors analyse with this methodical approach the within-country cross-sector comparative advantage of the UK, and the creative sector's backward and forward linkages to other sectors. For Germany, there is to my knowledge no systematic study of input-output linkages in the creative sector.

This is definitely a research topic to focus on, also as it applies to the study of value added chains and national accounts structures.

Last, but not least, in the literature and analyses on the creative sector, a missing link to innovation processes is found. Hardly any literature exists discussing the assumption that creativity is part of an innovation process. Exceptions are the works, for instance, from Georgieff et al. (2008), Hospers (2003), Mellander (2008), and Falk et al. (2011), who treat creativity as a part of an innovation process. In this context, innovation processes are *inter alia* a result of reciprocity, that is institutionalised forms of cooperation which includes cluster and networks of creative professionals. The organisational dimension of innovation within the creative sector are not reflected in the actual scientific work (for further discussions on organizational forms see Elsner et al. 2010). Since small and medium sized firms, open, flexible and new organisations as well as informal networks are assumed to dominate the creative sector, scientific research should focus on this organisational dimension. It would be useful to link to evolutionary process, especially in the context of interaction processes, emergent structures, i.e. trust, reciprocity and informal networks and institutions.

The job of urban economists, city planners or economic geographers is to make sense of all these unanswered questions and ideas to bring the science on urban and regional economics forward in the context of the creative economy. I hope this work inspires scholars and students working on the problems of the creative economy to pursue further research questions and to find beneficial answers through their scientific work.

A final remark. Lucas (1988) declared that knowledge spillovers through the clustering of human capital is one of the main reason for economic growth. Suedekum (2006, 2008), but also Florida (2002), followed this assumption. Suedekum (2006, 2008) developed a model to explain the employment growth coming from the clustering of high-skilled and low-skilled employment in a two-city model. Florida (2002) contributes to the discussion with the concept of the creative sector by developing his own human capital definition or, to be more precisely, measure based on an occupational classification. Regarding the aspect of measuring human capital, the results at hand are interesting since the concepts differ fundamentally.

Cities are generally in competition for human resources. Knowledge has become a predominant and competitive factor for economic development and welfare. Urban policy makers can attract human resources using different measures, like the promotion of cities as cultural centres or consumer cities. An important urban policy is also to invest in capital. The most valuable and important capital of all, however, is that which is invested in human resources (see, for example, also List 1925; Marshall 1920b). This investment forms the creative and knowledge economy. Both the creative and knowledge economy are linked to innovation, economic and employment growth. The work's results show that employment growth is not necessarily about new cutting edge technologies. However, this is not the full story on urban and regional employment growth, it is rather a multifaceted phenomenon that incorporates, *inter alia*, firms, institutional settings, problem-solving co-operations, and collective behaviour.

Bibliography

Acs. Z.. Audretsch. D.. Braunerhjelm. P. and Carlsson. B. (2004). *The missing link: The knowledge filter and entrepreneurship in endogenous growth*. Discussion Papers on Entrepreneurship. Growth and Public Policy 0805. Max Planck Institute for Research into Economic Systems (MPI). Jena.

Alesina. A. and Ferrara. E. L. (2005). Ethnic diversity and economic performance. *Journal of Economic Literature* **43**(7): 762 800.

Andersen. K. V. and Lorenzen. M. (2005). *The geography of the Danish creative class: A mapping and analysis*. imagine - Creative Industries Research. Copenhagen Business School (CBS). Frederiksberg.

Asheim. B. (1996). Industrial districts as "learning regions": A condition for prosperity. *European Planning Studies* **4**(4): 379 400.

Asheim. B. and Hansen. H. K. (2008). The creative class. people climate and business climate: Knowledge bases. varieties of capitalism and social capital. *in* H. K. Hansen (ed.). *The Urban Turn and the Location of Economic Activities*. Lund University. Lund. pp. 227 259.

Audretsch. D.. Dohse. D. and Niebuhr. A. (2009). Cultural diversity and entrepreneurship: A regional analysis for Germany. *The Annals of Regional Science* . DOI: 10.1007/s00168-009-0291-x.

Barrow. R. J. (1991). Economic growth in a cross-section of countries. *Quarterly Journal of Economics* **106**(2): 407 443.

Baycan-Levent. T. (2010). Diversity and creativity as seedbeds for urban and regional dynamics. *European Planning Studies* **18**(4): 565 594.

Becker. G. S. (1975). *Human capital: A theoretical and empirical analysis, with special reference to education*. Vol. o. 2 edn. National Bureau of Economic Research. New York.

Bellini. E.. Ottaviano. G. I.. Pinelli. D. and Prarolo. G. (2008). *Cultural diversity and economic performance: Evidence from European regions*. HWWI Research Papers 3-14. Hamburg Institute of International Economics (HWWI). Hamburg.

Besecke, A., Haselbach. D., Henckel. D., Mundelius, M., Pätzold. R. and Vosse, C. (2008). Kulturwirtschaft in Berlin: Entwicklungen und Potenziale. *Technical report*, Senatsverwaltung für Wirtschaft, Technologie und Frauen. Der Regierende Bürgermeister von Berlin, Senatskanzlei für kulturelle Angelegenheiten. Senatsverwaltung für Stadtentwicklung. Berlin.

Boje, A., Ott, I. and Stiller, S. (2010). Metropolitan cities under transition: The example of hamburg/germany. *Managing Global Transitions* **8**(4): 327–352.

Boschma, R. and Fritsch, M. (2007). Creative class and regional growth: Empirical evidence from seven European countries. *Economic Geography* **85**(4): 391–423.

Bundesagentur für Arbeit [Federal Employment Agency] (2007). Sozialversicherungspflichtige Beschäftigung und Erwerbstätigkeit: Entwicklung und Struktur 2000-2007, Nuremberg. [Official statistical data].

Bundesagentur für Arbeit [Federal Employment Agency] (2010). Sozialversicherungspflichtig Beschäftigte nach Wirtschaftsgruppen (WZ 2008). Nuremberg. [Official statistical data].

Cantner, U. (2000). Die Bedeutung von Innovationssystemen für die internationale Wettbewerbsfähigkeit, *in* U. Staroske. M. Wiegand-Kottisch and K. Wohlmuth (eds), *Innovation als Schlüsselfaktor eines erfolgreichen Wirtschaftsstandortes: Nationale und regionale Innovationssysteme im globalen Wettbewerb*, LIT-Verlag, Munster and Hamburg. pp. 77–110.

Chantelot, S., Peres, S. and Virol, S. (2010). *The geography of French creative class: An exploratory spatial data analysis*, Cahiers du GREThA Paper 16, Université Montesquieu Bordeaux. Bordeaux.

Damelang, A., Steinhardt, M. F. and Stiller, S. (2007). *Europe's diverse labour force: The case of German cities*, EURODIV PAPER 49, Fondazione Eni Enrico Mattei (FEEM). Milan.

David, P. A. (1985). Clio and the economics of qwerty. *The American Economic Review* **75**(2): 332–337.

De Hoyos, R. and Sarafidis. V. (2006). Testing for cross-sectional dependence in panel-data models. *The Stata Journal* **6**(4): 482–496.

dos Santos-Duisenberg, E., Joffe, A., Askerud, P., Fonseca-Reis. A. C., Diaz-Benevides, D. and Amaya-Londoño, S. (2008). Creative economy report 2008. The challenge of assessing the creative economy: Towards informed policy-making. *Report*, United Nations Conference on Trade and Development (UNCTAD). Geneva.

Drews, N. (2006). *Qualitätsverbesserung der Bildungsvariable in der IAB Beschäftigten-stichprobe 1975-2001*, number 5/2006, Nuremberg Research Data Centre (FDZ) of the Federal Employment Agency at the Institute for Employment Research, Nuremberg.

Drews, N. (2008). *Das Regionalfile der IAB-Beschäftigtenstichprobe 1975-2004: Hand-buchversion 1.0.2*, number 2/2008, Nuremberg Research Data Centre (FDZ) of the Federal Employment Agency at the Institute for Employment Research, Nuremberg.

Drews, N., Groll, D. and Jacobebbinghaus, P. (2007). *Programmierbeispiele zur Aufbere-itung von FDZ Personendaten in STATA*, number 6/2007, Nuremberg Research Data Centre (FDZ) of the Federal Employment Agency at the Institute for Employment Research, Nuremberg.

Driscoll, J. and Kraay, A. (1995). *Spatial correlations in panel data*, Policy Research Working Paper 1553, The World Bank.

Duranton, G. and Puga, D. (2000). Diversity and specialisation in cities: Why, where and when does it matter?, *Urban Studies* **37**(3): 533–555.

Duranton, G. and Puga, D. (2001). Nursery cities: Urban diversity, process innovation, and the life of cycle of products, *The American Economic Review* **91**(5): 1454–1477.

Elsner, W. (2000). An industrial policy agenda 2000 and beyond: Experience, theory and policy, *in* W. Elsner and J. Groenewegen (eds), *Industrial policies after 2000*, Kluwer Academic Publishers, Boston et al.

Elsner, W. (2004). The 'new' economy: complexity, coordination and a hybrid governance approach, *International Journal of Social Economics* **31**(11/12): 1029–1049.

Elsner, W. (2005). Real-world economics today: The new complexity, co-ordination and policy, *Review of Social Economy* **63**(1): 19–53.

Elsner, W. and Hanappi, H. (eds) (2008). *Varieties of capitalism and new institutional deals: Regulation, welfare and the new economy*, Edgar Elgar, Cheltenham et al.

Elsner, W. and Heinrich, T. (2009). A simple theory of meso: On the co-evolution of institutions and platform-size - With an application to varities of capitalism and medium-sized countries, *The Journal of Socio-Economics* **38**(5): 843–858.

Elsner, W., Hocker, G. and Schwardt, H. (2010). Simplistic vs. complex organization: Markets, hierarchies, and networks in an organizational triangle - A simple Heuristic to analyze real-world organizational forms, *Journal of Economic Issue* **44**(1): 1–29.

Evans, G. (2006). Strategies for creative spaces: London case study, *Commissioned report*, A report prepared for the London Development Agency (Creative London and the Evidence & Evaluation Team), the City of Toronto Economic Development and Culture offices, and the Ontario Ministries of Research & Innovation and Culture, London.

Evans, G. and Witting, A. (2006). Strategies for creative spaces: Berlin case study, *Commissioned report*. A report prepared for the London Development Agency (Creative London and the Evidence & Evaluation Team), the City of Toronto Economic Development and Culture offices, and the Ontario Ministries of Research & Innovation and Culture, London.

Falck, O., Fritsch, M. and Heblich, S. (2009). *Bohemians, human capital, and regional economic growth*, CESifo Working Paper 2715, Center for Economic Studies (CES), Institute for Economic Research (ifo) and the Munich Society for the Promotion of Economic Research (CESifo GmbH), Munich.

Falk, R., Bakhshi, H., Falk, M., Geiger, W., Karr, S., Keppel, C., Leo, H. and Spitzlinger, R. (2011). Innovation and competitiveness of the creative industries, *Commissioned report*, Österreichisches Institut für Wirtschaftsforschungs im Auftrag der Europäischen Kommission, DG Enterprise and Industry, Vienna.

FDZ (2008). IAB Regionalfile 1975-2004 (IABS-R04), Nuremberg Research Data Centre (FDZ) of the Federal Employment Agency at the Institute for Employment Research, Nuremberg. [Official statistical data].

Federal Office for Building and Regional Planning (2004). Karte Raumordnungsregionen 1.1.2004, Berlin. [www.bbsr.bund.de: requested 20/10/2009; 3:40 PM] [Official statistical data].

Federal Office for Building and Regional Planning (2010). Indikatoren und Karten zur Raum- und Stadtentwicklung, Elektronische Ressource (INKAR), Bonn. [Official statistical data].

Fitzenberger, B., Osikominu, A. and Völter, R. (2005). *Imputation rules to improve the education variable in the IAB employment subsample*, number 3/2005, Nuremberg Research Data Centre (FDZ) of the Federal Employment Agency at the Institute for Employment Research, Nuremberg.

Florida, R. (2002). *The rise of the creative class and how it's transforming work, leisure, community, and everyday life*, Basic Books, New York.

Florida, R. (2003). Cities and the creative class, *City & Community* **2**(1): 3-19.

Florida, R. (2005). *Cities and the creative class*, Routledge, New York and London.

Florida, R. (2009). *How the crash will reshap America*, The Atlantic Online, Washington. March 2009 [requested 04/08/2009; 1:20 PM].

Florida, R., Mellander, C. and Stolarick, K. (2008). Inside the black box of regional development - human capital, the creative class and tolerance, *Journal of Economic Geography* **8**(5): 615-649.

Florida. R.. Mellander. C. and Stolarick. K. (2010). *Music scenes to music clusters: The economic geography of music in the U.S., 1970-2000*. CESIS Electronic Working Paper 219 - Centre of Excellence for Science and Innovation Studies (CESIS). Jönköping.

Florida. R. and Tinagli. I. (2004). *Europe in the creative age*. Vol. 1. Carnegie Mellon Software Industry Center and Demos. Pittsburgh and London.

Frank. B. and Mundelius. M. (2005). Kreativbranchen in Berlin, *DIW Wochenbericht* 72(44): 665 670.

Freeman. A. (2008). *Benchmarking and understanding London's Cultural and Creative Industries*. MPRA Paper 14776. Munich Personal RePEc Archive (MPRA). Munich.

Fritsch. M. and Slavtchev. V. (2009). How does industry specialization affect the efficiency of regional innovation systems?, *The Annals of Regional Science* . DOI: 10.1007/s00168-009-0292-9.

Fritsch. M. and Stützer. M. (2006). *Die Geografie der kreativen Klasse in Deutschland*. Freiberger Working Papers 11. TU Bergakademie Freiberg. Freiberg.

Gabe. T. and Abel. J. (2011). Specialized knowledge and the geographic concentration of occupations. *Journal of Economic Geography* pp. 1 19. DOI:10.1093/jeg/lbr006.

Gartner. H. (2005). *The imputation of wages above the contribution limit with the German IAB employment sample*. number 2/2005. Nuremberg Research Data Centre (FDZ) of the Federal Employment Agency at the Institute for Employment Research. Nuremberg.

Georgieff. P.. Kimpeler. S.. Müller. K. and Rammer. C. (2008). Beitrag der Creative Industries zum Innovationssystem am Beispiel Österreichs, *Commissioned report*. Endbericht zur Studie im Auftrag der Wirtschaftskammer Österreich arge creativ wirtschaft austria. Karlsruhe and Mannheim.

Geppert. K. and Gornig. M. (2010). More people, more jobs: Urban renaissance in Germany, *DIW Wochenbericht* 6(22): 173 181.

Gertler. M. S.. Florida. R.. Gates. G. and Vinodrai. T. (2002). Competing on creativity: Placing Ontario's cities in North American context, *Commissioned report*. A report prepared for the Ontario Ministry of Enterprise. Opportunity and Innovation and the Institute for Competitiveness and Prosperity. Ontario.

Gertler. M. S.. Tesolin. L. and Weinstock. S. (2006). Strategies for creative cities project: Toronto case study. *Commissioned report*. A report prepared for the London Development Agency (Creative London and the Evidence & Evaluation Team). the City of Toronto Economic Development and Culture offices, and the Ontario Ministries of Research & Innovation and Culture. Toronto.

Glaeser, E. L. (1994). Cities, information, and economic growh, *Cityscape* **1**(1): 9 47.

Glaeser, E. L. (2005). Review of Richard Florida's the rise of the creative class, *Regional Science and Urban Economics* **35**(5): 593 596.

Glaeser, E. L. (2008). *Cities, agglomeration and spatial equilibrium*, Oxford University Press, Oxford and New York.

Glaeser, E. L., Kallal, H. D., Scheinkman, J. A. and Shleifer, A. (1992). Growth in cities, *The Journal of Political Economy* **100**(6): 1126 1152.

Glaeser, E. L. and Saiz, A. (2004). The rise of the skilled city, *Brookings-Wharton Papers on Urban Affairs* **5**: 47 105.

Gülümser, A. A., Baycan-Levent, T. and Nijkamp, P. (2010). Measuring regional creative capacity: A literature review for rural-specific approaches, *European Planning Studies* **18**(4): 545 563.

Hafner, S., von Streit, A., Miosga, M., Schröder, F. and Siekermann, K. (2007). München: Standortfaktor Kreativität, *Commissioned report*, Department für Geographie, Ludwig-Maximilians-Universität München im Auftrag der Landeshauptstadt München, Referat für Arbeit und Wirtschaft, Munich.

Hall, P. A. and Soskice, D. (eds) (2004). *Varieties of capitalism: The institutional foundations of comparative advantage*, reprinted edn, Oxford University Press, Oxford et al.

Hamann, S., Krug, G., Köhler, M., Ludwig-Mayerhofer, W. and Hacket, A. (2004). *Die IAB-Regionalstichprobe 1975-2001: IABS-R01*, 55, Zentralarchiv für Empirische Sozialforschung, ZA-Information, Cologne.

Hansen, H. K. (2007). *Technology, talent and tolerance: The geography of the creative class in Sweden*, Rapporter och Notitser 169, Department of Social and Economic Geography, Lund University, Lund.

Hansen, H. K. (2008). *The urban turn and the location of economic activities*, Lund University, Lund.

Hansen, H. K., Vang, J. and Asheim, B. (2005). *The creative class and regional growth: Towards a knowledge based approach*, CIRCLE Electronic Working Paper Series 05-15, Centre for Innovation, Research and Competence in the Learning Economy (CIRCLE), Lund.

Hesse, M. and Lange, B. (2007). Kreative Industrien: Magma und Mantra der Berliner Stadtentwicklung, *Kommune, Forum für Politik, Ökonomie, Kultur* **2**: 64 68.

Hoechle, D. (2007). Robust standard errors for panel regressions with cross-sectional dependence. *The Stata Journal* **7**(3): 281 312.

Hospers, G. J. (2003). Creative cities in Europe. Urban competitiveness in the knowledge economy. *Intereconomics* **28**(5): 260 269.

Howells, J. (1999). Regional system of innovation?, *in* D. Achibugi, J. Howells and J. Michie (eds), *Innovation policy in a global economy*, Cambridge University Press, Cambridge, pp. 67 93.

Hunt, J. (2006). Staunching from East Germany: Age and the determinants of migration, *Journal of the European Economic Association* **4**(5): 1014 1037.

Initiative Neue Soziale Marktwirtschaft (2011). Schuldenatlas der öffentlichen Haushalte Deutschland. Berlin. [Official statistical data].

Jacobs, J. (1969). *The economy of cities*, 1 edn, Random House, New York.

Jacobs, J. (1992). *The death and life of great American cities [1961]*, 1 edn, Vintage Books, New York.

Keane, M. P. (2010). A structural perspective on the experimentalist school, *Journal of Economic Perspectives* **24**(2): 47 58.

Klotz, C. and Theis, G. (2010). Black Box Kreativität, *Kreativität trifft Stadt. Zum Verhältnis von Kunst, Kultur und Stadtentwicklung im Rahmen der IBA Hamburg*, IBA Hamburg GmbH, Berlin, pp. 16 27.

Könönen, A., Köster, R., Lenné, T., Reich, N., Rohde, O., Stiller, S. and Wedemeier, J. (2008). *Zukunftschance Kreativität - Entwicklungspotenziale von Städten im Ostseeraum*, PricewaterhouseCoopers AG WPG (PwC) and Hamburgisches WeltWirtschaftsInstitut gemeinnützige GmbH (HWWI), Frankfurt/Main.

Kröhnert, S., Morgenstern, A. and Klingholz, R. (2007). *Talent, Technologie und Tolerance - Wo Deutschland Zukunft hat*, 1 edn, Berlin-Institut für Bevölkerung und Entwicklung, Berlin.

Landry, C. (2006). *The creative city - A toolkit for urban innovators*, reprinted edn, Comedia and Earthscan, Near Stroud, London et al.

Lee, S. Y., Florida, R. and Acs, Z. J. (2004). Creativity and entrepreneurship: A regional analysis of new firm formation, *Regional Studies* **38**(8): 879 891.

Liebmann, H. and Robischon, T. (eds) (2003). *Städtische Kreativität - Potenzial für den Stadtumbau*, Institut für Regionalentwicklung und Strukturplanung e. V. and Schader-Stiftung, Erkner and Darmstadt.

List, F. (1925). *Das nationale System der politischen Ökonomie [1841]*, Cotta, Stuttgart.

Lorenzen, M. and Andersen, K. V. (2007). *The geography of the European creative class: A rank size analysis*, DRUID Working Paper 07-17, Danish Research Unit for Industrial Dynamics (DRUID), Aalborg and Copenhagen.

Lucas, R. E. (1988). On the mechanics of economic development, *Journal of Monetary Economics* **22**: 3–42.

Lundvall, B. A. (1996). *The social dimension of the learning economy*, DRUID Working Paper 96-1, Danish Research Unit for Industrial Dynamics (DRUID), Aalborg and Copenhagen.

Lundvall, B. A. (2002). *The university in the learning economy*, DRUID Working Paper 02-6, Danish Research Unit for Industrial Dynamics (DRUID), Aalborg and Copenhagen.

Lundvall, B. A. (ed.) (1992). *National systems of innovation: Towards a theory of innovation and interactive learning*, Pinter, London.

Marlet, G. and van Woerkens, C. (2004). *Skills and creativity in a cross-section of Dutch cities*, Discussion Paper 04-29, Tjalling C. Koopmans Research Institute and Utrecht School of Economics, Utrecht.

Marrocu, E. and Paci, R. (2010). *Education of just creativity: What matters most for economic performance?*, Crenos Working paper 10-31, Contributi di ricerca crenos (Crenos), Cagliari.

Marshall, A. (1920a). *Industry and trade*, 3 edn, Macmillan and Co, London.

Marshall, A. (1920b). *Principles of economics [1890]*, 8 edn, Macmillan and Co, London.

Maskell, P., Eskelinen, H., Hannibalsson, I., Malmberg, A. and Vatne, E. (1998). *Localised learning and regional development: Specialisation and prosperity in small open economies*, Routledge, London and New York.

Maskell, P. and Lorenzen, M. (2004a). The cluster as market organisation, *Urban Studies* **41**(5/6): 991–1009.

Maskell, P. and Lorenzen, M. (2004b). *Firms and markets, networks and clusters, traditional and creative industries*, DRUID Winter Conference Paper 2004, Danish Research Unit for Industrial Dynamics (DRUID), Aalborg and Copenhagen.

Mellander, C. (2008). *The wealth of urban regions. On the location of creative individuals and firms*, JIBS Dissertation Series 053, Jönköping International Business School (JIBS), Jönköping.

Mellander, C. and Florida. R. (2007). *The creative class or human capital? Explaining regional development in Sweden*. CESIS Electronic Working Paper Series 79, Centre of Excellence for Science and Innovation Studies (CESIS). Jönköping.

Mitteilung des Senats an die Bürgerschaft (2009). *Aufbau des Kreativwirtschaftsclusters Hamburg*. Drucksache19/3442 edn. Bürgerschaft der Freien und Hansestadt Hamburg. Hamburg. [19. Wahlperiode].

Mitteilung des Senats an die Bürgerschaft (2010). *Leitbild Hamburg: Wachsen mit Weitsicht*. Drucksache19/5474 edn. Bürgerschaft der Freien und Hansestadt Hamburg. Hamburg. [19. Wahlperiode].

Möller, J. and Tubadji. A. (2009). *The creative class, bohemians and local labor market performance: A mirco data panel study for Germany 1975-2004*. ZEW Discussion Paper 08-135. Centre for European Economic Research (ZEW). Mannheim.

Moretti, E. (2004). Estimating the social returns to higher education: Evidence from longitudinal and repeated cross-section data, *Journal of Econometrics* **121**(1/2): 175 212.

Mundelius. M. (2009). Einkommen in der Berliner Kreativbranche: Angestellte Künstler verdienen am besten. *DIW Wochenbericht* **76**(9): 138 143.

Murphy, K. M., Shleifer, A. and Vishny, R. W. (1991). The allocation of talent: Implications for growth, *Quarterly Journal of Economics* **106**(2): 503 530.

Niebuhr, A. (2006). *Migration and innovation: Does cultural diversity matter for regional R&D activity?*, HWWI Research Paper 3-1, Hamburg Institute of International Economics (HWWI). Hamburg.

Nijkamp, P., van Oirschot, G. and Oosterman, A. (1993). *Regional development and engineering creativity: an international comparision of science parks in a knowledge society*. Research Memorandum 70, Faculteit der Economische Wetenschappen en Econometrie, Vrije Universiteit Amsterdam. Amsterdam.

N.N. (2006). The economy of culture in Europe, *Commissioned report*. A report prepared for the European Commission (DG Education and Culture) by KEA European Affairs. Media Group (Turku School of Economics) and MKW Wirtschaftsforschung GmbH. Brussels.

Oesch, D. and Menes, J. R. (2010). Upgrading or polarization? Occupational change in Britian, Germany, Spain, and Switzerland, 1990-2008. *Socio-Economic Review* **1**: 1 29. DOI:10.1093/ser/mwq029.

Ottaviano, G. I. and Peri, G. (2004). *Cities and cultures*. FEEM Working Paper 92. Fondazion Eni Enrico Mattei (FEEM). Milan.

Ottaviano, G. I. and Peri, G. (2006). The economic value of cultural diversity: Evidence from US cities, *Journal of Economic Geography* **6**(1): 9–44.

Overmeyer, K., Lange, B., Müller, C. and Spars, G. (2010). Kreative Milieus und offene Räume, *Commissioned report*, Studio UC im Auftrag für die Freie und Hansestadt Hamburg, Behörde für Stadtentwicklung und Umwelt, Amt für Landes- und Landschaftsplanung, Hamburg.

Peck, J. (2005). Struggling with the creative class, *International Journal of Urban and Regional Research* **29**(4): 740–770.

Pohl, T. (2008). Distribution patterns of the creative class in Hamburg: Openness to diversity as a driving force for socio-spatial differentiation?, *Erdkunde* **62**(4): 317–328.

Porter, M. E. (1998). Cluster and the new economics of competition, *Harvard Business Review* **Reprint 98609**: 73–91.

Quigley, J. M. (1998). Urban diversity and economic growth, *Journal of Economic Perspectives* **12**(2): 127–138.

Rauch, J. E. (1993). Productivity gains from geographic concentration of human capital: Evidence from the cities, *Journal of Urban Economics* **34**: 380–400.

Regional Account VGR der Laender (2007). Bruttoinlandsprodukt, Bruttowertschöpfung in den kreisfreien Städten und Landkreisen Deutschlands 1992 und 1994 bis 2006, Reihe 2, Band 1, Arbeitskreis "Volkswirtschaftliche Gesamtrechnungen der Länder" im Auftrag der Statistischen Ämter der 16 Bundesländer, des Statistischen Bundesamtes und des Bürgeramtes, Statistik und Wahlen, Frankfurt/Main. [Official statistical data].

Roback, J. (1982). Wages, rents, and the quality of life, *The Journal of Political Economy* **90**(6): 1257–1278.

Romer, P. M. (1990). Endogenous technological change, *Journal of Political Economy* **98**(5, Part 2): S71–S102.

Sassen, S. (2001). *The global city: New York, London, Tokyo*, 2 edn, Princeton University Press, Princeton and Oxford.

Schlitte, F. (2010). *Local human capital, segregation by skill, and skill-specific employment growth*, HWWI Research Paper 1-32, Hamburg Institute of International Economics (HWWI), Hamburg.

Schumpeter, J. (1950). *Kapitalismus, Sozialismus und Demokratie*, 7 edn, UTB, Tübingen and Basel.

Shaprio, J. M. (2006). Smart cities: Quality of life, productivity, and the growth effects of human capital, *The Review of Economics and Statistics* **88**(2): 324–335.

Smith. A. (2003). *Der Wohlstand der Nationen [1789]*. 10 edn. dtv. Munich. Auflage der Deutschen Übersetzung von 1978.

Söndermann. M. (2009). Leitfaden zur Erstellung einer statistischen Datengrundlage für die Kulturwirtschaft und eine länderübergreifende Auswertung kulturwirtschaftlicher Daten. *Commissioned report*. Büro für Kulturwirtschaftsforschung (KWF) im Auftrag der Ad-hoc-Arbeitsgruppe Kulturwirtschaft der Wirtschaftsministerkonferenz vertreten durch die Länder: Baden-Württemberg. Berlin. Brandenburg. Mecklenburg-Vorpommern. Niedersachsen. Nordrhein-Westfalen und Schleswig-Holstein. Cologne.

Söndermann. M.. Backes. C.. Arndt. O. and Brünink. D. (2009). Kultur- und Kreativwirtschaft: Ermittlung der gemeinsamen charakteristischen Definitionselemente der heterogenen Teilbereiche der Kulturwirtschaft zur Bestimmung ihrer Perspektiven aus volkswirtschaftlicher Sicht. *Commissioned report*. Creative Business Consult (CBC). Büro für Kulturwirtschaftsforschung (KWF) und prognos AG im Auftrag des Bundesministeriums für Wirtschaft und Technologie (BMWI). Cologne. Bremen and Berlin.

Storper. M. and Scott. A. J. (2009). Rethinking human capital, creativity and urban growth. *Journal of Economic Geography* 9(2): 147–167.

Storper. M. and Venables. A. J. (2004). Buzz: Face-to-face contact and the urban economy. *Journal of Economic Geography* 4(4): 351–370.

Studenmund. A. H. (2006). *Using econometrics: A practical guide*, 5 edn. Pearson International Edition. Boston et al.

Suedekum. J. (2006). *Human capital externalities and growth of high- and low-skilled jobs*. IZA Discussion Paper 1969. Institute for the Study of Labor (IZA). Bonn.

Suedekum. J. (2008). Convergence of the skill composition across German regions. *Regional Science and Urban Economics* 38(2): 148–159.

Suedekum. J. (2010). Human capital externalities and growth of high- and low-skilled jobs. *Jahrbücher für Nationalökonomie und Statistik* 230(1): 92–114.

Thierstein. A. and Goebel. V. (2007). Das maritime Bild der Region Hamburg. *RegionPol. Zeitschrift für Regionalwirtschaft* 1: 23–29.

Tobler. W. R. (1970). A computer movie simulating urban growth in the Detroit region. *Economic Geography* 46(2): 234–240.

Traxler. J.. Grossgasteiger. S.. Kurzmann. R.. Ploder. M.. Behr. M.. Gigler. C.. Müller. W.. Niegelhell. F.. Schirmbacher. B.. Sittinger. E.. Wildner. W. and Horx. M. (2006). creative: graz. Potenzialanalyse Kreativwirtschaft im Grossraum Graz. *Commissioned*

report, Joanneum Research Forschungsgesellschaft mbH und Institut für Technologie-
und Regionalpolitik im Auftrag des Landesrates für Wirtschaft und Innovation, Dr.
Christian Buchmann, des Stadtrates für Wirtschaft, Tourismus und Sport, Detlev Eisel-
Eiselsberg, des Präsidenten der Wirtschaftskammer Steiermark, KoR Peter Mühlbacher,
Graz.

von Osten, M. (2008). Unberechenbare Ausgänge. *Kreativen:Wirkungen. Urbane Kultur,
Wissensökonomie und Stadtpolitik*, Vol. 2, Heinrich-Böll-Stiftung, Berlin.

Wedemeier, J. (2010a). *The impact of creativity on growth in German regions*, SUSDIV
PAPER 14-2010, Fondazione Eni Enrico Mattei (FEEM), Milan.

Wedemeier, J. (2010b). The impact of the creative sector on growth in German regions,
European Planning Studies **18**(4): 505–520.

Wedemeier, J. (2011). Creative cities and the concept of diversity, *in* F. Eckardt and
J. Eade (eds), *Ethnically Diverse City*, Berliner Wissenschaftsverlag, Berlin.

Wirtschaftsministerkonferenz (2009). *Beschluss der Wirtschaftsministerkonferenz am
14./15. Dezember 2009 in Lübeck. Punkt 9 der Tagesordnung: Kreativwirtschaft
- Verbesserung der Rahmenbedingungen für eine Wachstumsbranche*, Bundesrat,
Wirtschaftsministerkonferenz (WMK), Konferenz der Fachminister, Wirtschaft, Berlin.

Wojan, T. R., Lambert, D. M. and McGranahan, D. A. (2007). Emoting with their feet:
Bohemian attraction to creative milieu, *Journal of Economic Geography* **7**(6): 711–736.

Wooldridge, J. M. (2009). *Introductory econometrics: A modern approach*, 4 edn, South-
Western, Canada.

Wu, W. (2005). *Dynamic cities and creative clusters*, World Bank Policy Research Working Paper 3509, The World Bank, Washington.

Ye, Z. and Yin, Y. P. (2007). *Economic linkages and comparative advantage of the UK
creative sector*, UHBS Working Paper 2, University of Hertfordshire Business School
(UHBS), Hertfordshire.

A. Tables, figures, and test statistics

Contents

A.1. Tables

Table A.1.1: Florida's creative sector

Major professional categories

Super Creative Sector
    Computer and mathematical professionals
    Architecture and engineering professionals
    Life, physical and social science professionals
    Education, training, and library professionals
    Arts, design, entertainment, sports, and media professionals
Creative professionals
    Management professionals
    Business, financial operations, and legal professionals
    Healthcare practitioners and technical professionals
    High-end sales and sales management
Industry sector
    Construction and extraction professionals
    Installation, maintenance, and repair professionals
    Production, Transportation, and material moving professionals
Service sector
    Health care support professionals
    Food preparation and food service-related professionals
    Building and grounds cleaning and maintenance professionals
    Personal care, service, and protective service professionals
    Low-end sales and related professionals
    Office and administrative support professionals
    Community and social services professionals
Agriculture Sector
    Farming, fishing, and forestry professionals

Source: Florida (2002, pp. 328-329).

Table A.1.2: Summary of creative cities and regions literature

Region /	Methodology			Result
Analysed question	Talent	Technology	Tolerance	

Andersen and Lorenzen (2005)

38 Danish city regions and 273 municipalities / Where is the creative sector located? What determines the location? Connection to economic growth?	Creative sector index: - Creative core - Creative professional Bohemians	- Share of employed in high-tech industries - Business life growth	Local amenities: - Unemployed non-western citizens - Share of foreign western and non-western citizens - Cultural opportunities - Unemployment rate - Public provision	Local amenities affect the localisation of the creative sector. Creative sector is positively correlated with population, employment growth, the growth in the number of firms and the presence of high-tech employees.

Fritsch and Stützer (2006)

438 German districts / Where is the creative sector located? What determines the location? Connection to economic growth?	Creative sector index: - Creative core - Creative professionals	- Share of employees in R&D intensive manufacturing and knowledge intensive services - Start-up rate - Innovation index	Local amenities: - Public provision index - Share of foreigners in the total population - Population density - Share of bohemians - Employment growth	Creative people live in places with a high share of foreigners, public provision and cultural amenities. Creative sector is an important determinant of economic growth.

Hansen (2007)

81 Swedish labour market regions / Where is the creative sector located? What determines the location? Connection to economic growth?	Creative sector index: - Creative core - Creative professionals For dynamic analysis: - Share of population with bachelors degree	- Tech-Pole production - Formation of new firms	Local amenities: - Share of bohemians - Share of foreign-born in the population - Share of foreign-born non-western citizens - Share of foreign-born unemployment - Public provision - Cultural opportunity	Bohemians, but also, the public provision have a statistical significant influence on the location of the creative sector. Presence of creative sector has positive effect on technology. Dynamic models only bring about moderate values.

Table A.1.2: Summary of creative cities and regions literature (cont.)

Region /	Methodology			Result
Analysed question	Talent	Technology	Tolerance	

Kröhnert et al. (2007)

16 German Federal States / Where is the creative sector located? Measuring a trend index for future potential of technology, talent and tolerance.	Creative sector index: - Creative core - Share of people with tertiary education in a age of 20-59	- Gross expenditure on research and development - Patent applications - High-tech patent applications	- Share of bohemians - Share of vote for right wing parties - Share of foreigners in the population - Share of acceptance for xenophobic statements in the population	The three tolerance indicators are positively correlated with the location of the creative sector.

Möller and Tubadji (2009)

323 German districts / Does regional concentration of the creative sector perform better in employment or wage growth? Is the creative sector following the bohemians?	- Creative sector: - Bohemians, - Other Creative Core - Creative Professionals Further controls: - Share of high-skilled workers - share of workers in mathematics, engineering, natural sciences and techniques (MENT) - share of workers in humanities.	-	- Bohemians	Creative sector contributes to regional performance. Bohemians do not attract creative agents.

Table A.1.3: Definition of the creative sector (Definition 1)

Occupational title	IAB-Label
Agents with technological creative ability (technological employees)	
Mechanical and vehicle engineers.	63
Electrical engineers.	64
Architects and construction engineers.	65
Surveyors, mining, metallurgists and related engineers.	66
Miscellaneous engineers.	67
Chemists, physicists, chemical/physical engineers, mathematicians, and civil engineering technicians.	68
Mechanical engineering technicians.	69
Electrical engineers technicians.	70
Surveyors, chemical, physical, mining, metallurgists, and miscellaneous engineering technicians.	71
Miscellaneous technicians.	72
Biological/mathematical/physical-technical assistant, chemical and related laboratory technician workers.	74
Draft persons.	75
Computer related professions.	99
Statisticians, humanists, natural scientists, and pastors.	120
Agents with cultural creative ability (bohemians)	
Journalists, publishers, librarians, archivists, museum specialists.	107
Musicians, performing artists, performers, graphic artists, designers, decorators, sign painters, stage, image and audio engineers, photographers, artists, and professional athletes.	108

Table A.1.4: Definition of the creative class (Definition 2)

Occupational title	IAB-Label
Agents with technological creative ability (technological employees)	
Mechanical and vehicle engineers.	63
Electrical engineers.	64
Architects and construction engineers.	65
Surveyors, mining, metallurgists and related engineers.	66
Miscellaneous engineers.	67
Chemists, physicists, chemical/physical engineers, mathematicians, and civil engineering technicians.	68
Mechanical engineering technicians.	69
Electrical engineers technicians.	70
Surveyors, chemical, physical, mining, metallurgists, and miscellaneous engineering technicians.	71
Miscellaneous technicians.	72
Foreman, work master.	73
Biological/mathematical/physical-technical assistant, chemical and related laboratory technician workers.	74
Draft persons.	75
Software programmers, computer related professions.	99
Statisticians, humanists, natural scientists, and pastors.	120
Agents with economic creative ability	
Analysts, entrepreneurs, leading administration, opinion makers.	93-95
University professors, education.	118
Financial services.	80
Legal services, lawyers, officers, justice, and soldiers.	104
Agents with cultural creative ability (bohemians)	
Journalists, publishers, librarians, archivists, museum specialists.	107
Musicians, performing artists, performers, graphic artists, designers, decorators, sign painters, stage, image and audio engineers, photographers, artists, and professional athletes.	108

Table A.1.5: Definition of the skill groups (Definition 3)	
Educational title	IAB-Label
Low-skill	
Basic education, no vocational education.	1
Gymnasium, no vocational education.	3
Medium-Skill	
Basic education with vocational education.	2
Gymnasium with vocational education.	4
High-skill	
University of applied science.	5
University.	6

Table A.1.6: Distribution of creative professionals and skill groups (mean) by labour time (1977, 86, 95)

Creative sector	Others	TE	BOH	Total	
Part-time	112.715	3.307	833	116.855	
	11.25	3.84	9.63	10.65	
Full-time	889.237	82.907	7.813	979.957	
	88.75	96.16	90.37	89.35	
Total	1.001.952	86.214	8.646	1.096.812	
	100	100	100	100	
Creative class	Others	CC	BOH	Total	Key
Part-time	106.387	9.635	833	116.855	frequency
	11.46	6.02	9.63	10.65	col percent
Full-time	821.648	150.496	7.813	979.957	
	88.54	93.98	90.37	89.35	
Total	928.035	160.131	8.646	1.096.812	
	100	100	100	100	
Skill group	Low-skilled	Skilled	High-skilled	Total	
Part-time	31.571	78.218	7.066	116.855	
	13.89	9.89	8.98	10.65	
Full-time	195.742	712.583	71.632	979.957	
	86.11	90.11	91.02	89.35	
Total	227.313	790.801	78.698	1.096.812	
	100	100	100	100	

Source: IABS Regionalfile 1975-2004, FDZ (2008), own calculations.

Table A.1.7: Distribution of creative professionals (mean) by skill groups (1977, 86, 95)

	Low skilled	Skilled	High-skilled	Total
Creative sector				
Others	223,077	734.921	43.954	1.001.952
	22.26	73.35	4.39	100
	98.14	92.93	55.85	91.35
TE	3,601	49.958	32.655	86.214
	4.18	57.95	37.88	100
	1.58	6.32	41.49	7.86
BOH	635	5.922	2.089	8.646
	7.34	68.49	24.16	100
	0.28	0.75	2.65	0.79
Total	227.313	790.801	78.698	1.096.812
	20.72	72.10	7.18	100
	100	100	100	100
Florida's creative class				
Others	217.996	681.161	28.878	928.035
	23.49	73.40	3.11	100
	95.90	86.14	36.69	84.61
CC	8682	103.718	47.731	160.131
	5.42	64.77	29.81	100
	3.82	13.12	60.65	14.60
BOH	635	5.922	2.089	8.646
	7.34	68.49	24.16	100
	0.28	0.75	2.65	0.79
Total	227.313	790.801	78.698	1.096.812
	20.72	72.10	7.18	100
	100	100	100	100

Key

frequency
row percent
col percent

Source: IABS Regionalfile 1975-2004, FDZ (2008), own calculations.

Table A.1.8: Distribution of the creative sector by the *AGG* variable (1977. 04)

Year 1977	Others	TE	BOH	Total
AGG=0	128.165	6.934	768	135.867
	94.33	5.10	0.57	100
	39.72	30.14	30.55	39.02
AGG=1	194.544	16.074	1.746	212.364
	91.61	7.57	0.82	100
	60.28	69.86	69.45	60.98
Total	322.709	23.008	2.514	348.231
	92.67	6.61	0.72	100
	100	100	100	100

Year 2004					Key
AGG=0	167.518	13.309	1.210	182.037	frequency
	92.02	7.31	0.66	100	row percent
	43.00	33.77	30.88	42.05	col percent
AGG=1	222.090	26.106	2.708	250.904	
	88.52	10.40	1.08	100	
	57.00	66.23	69.12	57.95	
Total	389.608	39.415	3.918	432.941	
	89.99	9.10	0.90	100	
	100	100	100	100	

Growth 1977-2004				
AGG=0	26.78	65.20	45.46	29.25
AGG=1	13.24	48.50	43.89	16.68
Total	18.84	53.83	44.37	21.77

Notes: AGG=1 are regions with an employment concentration above the 70th percentile; AGG=1. 22 planning regions (1977 and 04); AGG=0, 52 planning regions (1977 and 04); Growth is calculated by $growth_t = ln(variable_t) - ln(variable_{t-1})$.
Source: IABS Regionalfile 1975-2004. FDZ (2008), own calculations.

Table A.1.9: Distribution of Florida's creative class by the AGG variable (1977, 04)

Year 1977	Others	CC	BOH	Total
AGG=0	120,480	14,619	768	135,867
	88.67	10.76	0.57	100
	40.01	32.81	30.55	39.02
AGG=1	180,679	29,939	1,746	212,364
	85.08	14.10	0.82	100
	59.99	67.19	69.45	60.98
Total	301,159	44,558	2,514	348,231
	86.48	12.80	0.72	100
	100	100	100	100

Year 2004					Key
AGG=0	156,268	24,559	1,210	182,037	frequency
	85.84	13.49	0.66	100	row percent
	43.57	34.92	30.88	42.05	col percent
AGG=1	202,422	45,774	2,708	250,904	
	80.68	18.24	1.08	100	
	56.43	65.08	69.12	57.95	
Total	358,690	70,333	3,918	432,941	
	82.85	16.25	0.90	100	
	100	100	100	100	

Growth 1977-2004				
AGG=0	26.01	51.88	45.46	29.25
AGG=1	11.36	42.46	43.89	16.68
Total	17.48	45.64	44.37	21.77

Notes: AGG=1 are regions with an employment concentration above the 70th percentile; AGG=1, 22 planning regions (1977 and 04); AGG=0, 52 planning regions (1977 and 04); Growth is calculated by $growth_t = ln(variable_t) - ln(variable_{t-1})$.
Source: IABS Regionalfile 1975-2004, FDZ (2008), own calculations.

Table A.1.10: Distribution of the high-skilled agents by the AGG variable (1977, 04)

Year 1977	Low-skilled	Skilled	High-skilled	Total	Key
AGG=0	34.940	95.864	5.063	135.867	
	25.72	70.56	3.73	100	
	41.73	38.78	29.33	39.02	
AGG=1	48.796	151.366	12.202	212.364	
	22.98	71.28	5.75	100	
	58.27	61.22	70.67	60.98	
Total	83.736	247.230	17.265	348.231	
	24.05	71.00	4.96	100	
	100	100	100	100	
Year 2004					**Key**
AGG=0	36.004	131.874	14.159	182.037	frequency
	19.78	72.44	7.78	100	row percent
	45.25	42.73	31.65	42.05	col percent
AGG=1	43.557	176.767	30.580	250.904	
	17.36	70.45	12.19	100	
	54.75	57.27	68.35	57.95	
Total	79.561	308.641	44.739	432.941	
	18.38	71.29	10.33	100	
	100	100	100	100	
Growth 1977-2004					
AGG=0	3.00	31.89	102.84	29.25	
AGG=1	-11.36	15.51	91.87	16.68	
Total	-5.11	22.19	95.22	21.77	

Notes: AGG=1 are regions with an employment concentration above the 70th percentile;
AGG=1, 22 planning regions (1977 and 04); AGG=0, 52 planning regions (1977 and 04);
Growth is calculated by $growth_t = ln(variable_t) - ln(variable_{t-1})$.
Source: IABS Regionalfile 1975-2004. FDZ (2008), own calculations.

Table A.1.11: Definition of the cultural and creative sector

Cultural and creative sector	WZ-label (1)
Publishing	22.1
Motion pictures and video	92.1
Radio and television	92.2
Cultural activities	92.3
Journalist and newcast	92.4
Library and museums	92.5
Trade with cultural goods	52.45.3, 52.47.2, 52.48.2
Architecture	74.20.1, 74.20.2, 74.20.3
Design (2)	74.20.6, 74.87.4, 74.40.1
Advertisement (2)	74.40.1, 74.40.2
Software and Games	72.2

Notes: Employees who are subject to compulsory insurance deductions; (1) Wirtschaftszweigklassifikation (WZ) 2008, WZ-Number 3 and 5; (2) with double count (WZ-label 74.40.1).
Source: Bundesagentur für Arbeit [Federal Employment Agency] (2010), definition of the cultural and creative sector based on Söndermann (2009); Wirtschaftsministerkonferenz (2009).

Table A.1.12: Cultural and creative sector employment (2003)

	Hamburg			Berlin			Munich		
	total	share of		total	share of		total	share of	
Submarket (1)		(2)	(3)		(2)	(3)		(2)	(3)
Publishing	13,942	22.3	1.6	7,719	11.8	0.6	11,529	20.6	1.5
Motion pictures	3,293	5.3	0.4	7,288	11.1	0.6	4,087	7.3	0.5
Radio/television	6,331	10.1	0.7	4,993	7.6	0.4	4,914	8.8	0.6
Cultural activities	5,196	8.3	0.6	9,377	14.3	0.8	4,491	8.0	0.6
Journalist	1,187	1.9	0.1	1,505	2.3	0.1	564	1.0	0.1
Library/museums	1,849	3.0	0.2	4,010	6.1	0.3	2,186	3.9	0.3
Trade with cultural goods	2,564	4.1	0.3	2,657	4.1	0.2	2,937	5.2	0.4
Architecture	2,857	4.6	0.3	5,137	7.8	0.4	3,345	6.0	0.4
Design (4)	8,970	14.3	1.0	5,602	8.6	0.5	5,445	9.7	0.7
Advertising (4)	12,453	19.9	1.4	8,206	12.5	0.7	6,368	11.4	0.8
Software/Games	12,246	19.6	1.4	14,140	21.6	1.2	14,990	26.8	1.9
Cultural/creative sector (5)	62,580	100	7.2	65,515	100	5.4	55,970	100	7.2

Notes: Employees who are subject to compulsory insurance deductions, ; (1) Wirtschaftszweigklassifikation (WZ) 2008, WZ-Number 3 and 5, see also A.1.11 in the appendix; (2) creative economy; (3) overall economy; (4) with double count; (5) without double count.
Source: Bundesagentur für Arbeit [Federal Employment Agency] (2010), definition based on Söndermann (2009); Wirtschaftsministerkonferenz (2009), own calculations.

A.2. Figures

Figure A.2.1: Creative class and wage (1977, 86, 95)

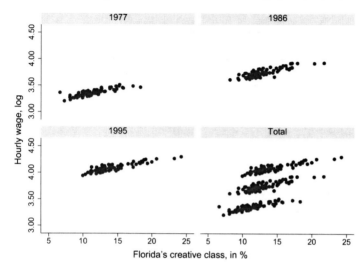

Florida's creative class, in %

Notes: year 1977: $R^2 = 70.13$ percent, p-value=0.000, N=74; year 1986: $R^2 = 68.79$ percent, p-value=0.000, N=74; year 1995: $R^2 = 76.43$ percent, p-value=0.000, N=74
Source: IABS Regionalfile 1975-2004, FDZ (2008), own calculations.

Figure A.2.2: High-skilled agents and wage (1977, 86, 95)

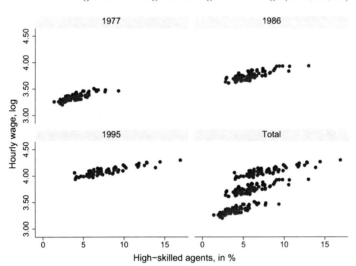

Notes: year 1977: R^2 = 62.83 percent, p-value=0.000, N=74; year 1986: R^2 = 63.16 percent, p-value=0.000, N=74; year 1995: R^2 = 74.08 percent, p-value=0.000, N=74
Source: IABS Regionalfile 1975-2004, FDZ (2008), own calculations.

Figure A.2.3: Planning regions (2004)

Notes: Figure's numbers are explained on the following page.
Source: Federal Office for Building and Regional Planning (2004).

Figure A.2.3: Planning regions (2004) (cont.)

1 Schleswig-Holstein Nord	34 Halle/S.	67 Saar
2 SH Süd-West	35 Münster	68 Unterer Neckar
3 SH Mitte	36 Bielefeld	69 Franken
4 SH Ost	37 Paderborn	70 Mittlerer Oberrhein
5 SH Süd	38 Arnsberg	71 Nordschwarzwald
6 Hamburg	39 Dortmund	72 Stuttgart
7 Westmecklenburg	40 Emscher-Lippe	73 Ostwürttemberg
8 Mittleres Mecklenburg	41 Duisburg/Essen	74 Donau-Iller (BW)
9 Vorpommern	42 Düsseldorf	75 Neckar-Alb
10 Mecklenburg-Seenplatte	43 Bochum/Hagen	76 Baar-Heuberg
11 Bremen	44 Köln	77 Südlicher Oberrhein
12 Ostfriesland	45 Aachen	78 Hochrhein-Bodensee
13 Bremerhaven	46 Bonn	79 Oberschwaben
14 Hamburg-Umland-Süd	47 Siegen	80 Bayerischer/Main
15 Bremen-Umland	48 Nordhessen	81 Würzburg
16 Oldenburg	49 Mittelhessen	82 Main-Rhön
17 Emsland	50 Osthessen	83 Oberfranken-West
18 Osnabrück	51 Rhein-Main	84 Oberfranken-Ost
19 Hannover	52 Starkenburg	85 OberpfalzNord
20 Südheide	53 Nordthüringen	86 Mittelfranken
21 Lüneburg	54 Mittelthüringen	87 Westmittelfranken
22 Braunschweig	55 Südthüringen	88 Augsburg
23 Hildesheim	56 Ostthüringen	89 Ingolstadt
24 Göttingen	57 Westsachsen	90 Regensburg
25 Prignitz-Oberhavel	58 Osterzgebirge	91 Donau-Wald
26 Uckermark-Barnim	59 Oberlausitz	92 Landshut
27 Oderland-Spree	60 Chemnitz	93 München
28 Lausitz-Spreewald	61 Südwestsachsen	94 Donau-Iller (BY)
29 Havelland-Fläming	62 Westerwald	95 Allgäu
30 Berlin	63 Trier	96 Oberland
31 Altmark	64 Rheinhessen	97 Südostoberbayern
32 Magdeburg	65 Westpfalz	
33 Dessau	66 Rheinpfalz	

Source: Federal Office for Building and Regional Planning (2004).

A.3. Test statistics

Table A.3.1: Test statistics, total employment effects

Creative sector: Definition 1

Test statistics panel analysis for fixed effects
Joint test on significance $F(73, 140) = 3.32$ Prob>F = 0.000
Breusch-Pagan-LM test   chi2(9) = 25.818   Prob>chi2 = 0.022
Hausman test   chi2(8) = 552.18   Prob>chi2 = 0.000
Test cross-sectional dependence and heteroscedasticity
Pesaran's test   = 3.924   Prob (>=0) = 0.000
   Average absolute value = 0.685
Wald test   chi2(74) = 230000.00   Prob>chi2 = 0.000

Florida's creative class: Definition 2

Test statistics panel analysis for fixed effects
Joint test on significance $F(73, 140) = 3.26$ Prob>F = 0.000
Breusch-Pagan-LM test   chi2(9) = 21.215   Prob>chi2 = 0.012
Hausman test   chi2(8) = 518.57   Prob>chi2 = 0.000
Test cross-sectional dependence and heteroscedasticity
Pesaran's test   = 5.696   Prob (>=0) = 0.000
   Average absolute value = 0.676
Wald test   chi2(74) = 7674.92   Prob>chi2 = 0.000

High-skilled agents: Definition 3

Test statistics panel analysis for fixed effects
Joint test on significance $F(73, 140) = 6.08$ Prob>F = 0.000
Breusch-Pagan-LM test   chi2(9) = 16.737   Prob>chi2 = 0.053
Hausman test   chi2(8) = 610.81   Prob>chi2 = 0.000
Test cross-sectional dependence and heteroscedasticity
Pesaran's test   = -0.529   Prob (>=0) = 1.403
   Average absolute value = 0.657
Wald test   chi2(74) = 5830000.00   Prob>F = 0.000

Source: IABS Regionalfile 1975-2004, FDZ (2008), own calculations.

Table A.3.2: Test statistics, groups specific employment effects

Creative sector: Definition 1

Test statistics panel analysis for fixed effects
  Joint test on significance $F(73, 140) = 2.42$ $Prob>F = 0.000$
  Breusch-Pagan-LM test $chi2(9) = 14.30$ $Prob>chi2 = 0.112$
  Hausman test $chi2(8) = 29.64$ $Prob>chi2 = 0.000$
Test cross-sectional dependence and heteroscedasticity
  Pesaran's test $= 2.293$ $Prob\ (>=0) = 0.022$
                                Average absolute value $= 0.633$
  Wald test $chi2(74) = 150000.00$ $Prob>chi2 = 0.000$

Florida's creative class: Definition 2

Test statistics panel analysis for fixed effects
  Joint test on significance $F(73, 140) = 4.43$ $Prob>F = 0.000$
  Breusch-Pagan-LM test $chi2(17) = 21.38$ $Prob>chi2 = 0.011$
  Hausman test $chi2(9) = 101.32$ $Prob>chi2 = 0.000$
Test cross-sectional dependence and heteroscedasticity
  Pesaran's test $= -0.615$ $Prob\ (>=0) = 0.539$
                                Average absolute value $= 0.650$
  Wald test $chi2(74) = 15000000.00$ $Prob>chi2 = 0.000$

High-skilled agents: Definition 3

Test statistics panel analysis for fixed effects
  Joint test on significance $F(73, 140) = 1.39$ $Prob>F = 0.047$
  Breusch-Pagan-LM test $chi2(9) = 73.694$ $Prob>chi2 = 0.000$
  Hausman test $chi2(8) = 40.16$ $Prob>chi2 = 0.000$
Test autocorrelation and heteroscedasticity
  Pesaran's test $= -1.165$ $Prob\ (>=0) = 1.756$
                                Average absolute value $= 0.638$
  Wald test $chi2 = 1500000.00$ $Prob>F= 0.000$

Source: IABS Regionalfile 1975-2004, FDZ (2008), own calculations.

The Book Series
‚Structural Change and Structural Policies'

'Structural change', and particularly 'global' structural change, is a ubiquitous and topical issue. Indeed, it is the phenomenon that reflects the *dynamics* and *complex evolution* of the economy most immediately and comprehensively—and, in turn, is at the basis of economic growth and evolution. Also, economic policy has become much more 'structural policy', or better: a whole spread of 'structural policies', in recent decades, rather than just aggregate or macro management.

Viewed *statically* and *statistically*, 'structure' and 'structural change' mirror socio-economic phenomena simply at a *'middle' range of aggregation*: *Industries*, sectors, branches, industrial-spatial *clusters* and firm *networks*, furthermore *regions*, and, finally, statistical *size ranges of firms* (the class of mini and 'micro' units, including spin-offs or new firm start-ups, further the renowned 'small and medium-sized firms' group or layer, up to the large companies and the 'transnational corporations', another research area of its own). Corresponding structural policies would comprise *industrial policies*, including nowadays a broad support for *start-ups* and 'entrepreneurship', *cluster-* and *network*-oriented development strategies as well as related *innovation* policy and some '*human capital*' development policy. They also contain *regional policies*, again today mostly cluster- and network-based, sometimes aiming at *spatially even* living conditions and regional *convergence*, sometimes aiming at strengthening the strong *metropolitan growth centres* (mostly pursuing both of these contradictory objectives at a time, though).

This series, basically, is designed to contribute to the different aspects, areas, and questions mentioned of *modern 'interactive' meso-economics*. Conventional *microeconomics* appears highly insufficient against the background indicated, and *macroeconomics* still needs reliable 'micro-foundations', which will need to be *micro-* and *'meso'-foundations*. In terms of policy, there are manifold and ubiquitous *unintended 'structural' consequences* of spontaneous both micro and macro processes, and of conventional both micro- and macro policies. The remedies are supposed to lie in more adequate, theoretically better informed, and well-designed structures of private-private and private-public interactions, at micro, 'meso', and macro levels.

Wolfram Elsner,
University of Bremen, Germany
Managing Editor: Dr. Henning Schwardt

Band 6 Martin Wrobel: Flughäfen in der Region. Regionale Gravitationszentren vor dem Verkehrsinfarkt? Eine Strukturanalyse und Prognose der landseitigen Verkehrssituation – am Beispiel des Airport Bremen. 2002.

Band 7 Martin Heinlein: Innovationen kleiner Unternehmen in regionalen Netzwerken. Die Förderung von Forschung und Entwicklung durch aktive Vermittlung im Wissens- und Technologietransfer. 2004.

Band 8 Martin Wrobel: Die Logistik als Motor regionaler Strukturentwicklung. Sektorale Clusterstrukturen und Netzwerkpotentiale am Beispiel Bremen und Hamburg. 2004.

Band 9 Sabine Bruns-Vietor: Logistik, Organisation und Netzwerke. Eine radikal konstruktivistische Diskussion des Fließsystemansatzes. 2004.

Band 10 Ernst Mönnich: Erklärungsansätze regionaler Entwicklung und politisches Handeln. Kritik und regionalökonomische Konsequenzen. 2004.

Band 11 Jost Bartkowiak: Stadtzentren im Umbruch. Zur *Revitalisierung* von Großstadtzentren, deren Bedeutung für Stadtökonomie, Städtebau und Stadtgesellschaft. Am Beispiel zentralstädtischer Bahnhofsareale. 2004.

Band 12 Wolfram Elsner / Christoph Otte / Inhi Yu: Klimawandel und regionale Wirtschaft. Vermögensschäden und Einkommensverluste durch extreme Klimaereignisse sowie Kosten-Nutzen-Analysen von Schutzmaßnahmen. Am Beispiel der nordwestdeutschen Küstenregion. 2005.

Band 13 Wolfram Elsner / J. Andreas Hübscher / Manfred Zachcial: Regionale Logistik-Cluster. Statistische Erfassung, Stärken und Schwächen, Handlungspotentiale. 2005.

Band 14 Marion Salot: Konkurrenz und Kooperation in Hightech-Branchen. Das Beispiel der internationalen Flugzeugbauindustrie. 2006.

Band 15 Maya Behrens-Schablow: Unternehmensinterne Netzwerke in der Informationsgesellschaft. Prozesse und Gestaltung der Vernetzung, Netzwerkkultur und Social Learning am Beispiel der Einführung von DC eLife in der DaimlerChrysler AG. 2007.

Band 16 Stefan Reiter: Wettbewerb und Monopolisierung in der Luft- und Raumfahrtindustrie. Analyse und Bewertung des Unternehmenszusammenschlusses Daimler-Benz/MBB aus Sicht der modernen Industrieökonomik. 2007.

Band 17 Lorraine Frisina: Understanding Regional Development. Absorption, Institutions and Socioeconomic Growth in the Regions of the European Union. A Case Study on Italy. 2008.

Band 18 Gero Hocker: Market – Hierarchy – Networking: Cooperation in Times of Globalization, Fragmentation, and Uncertainty. 2008.

Band 19 Bernhard Dachs: Innovative Activities of Multinational Enterprises in Austria. 2009.

Vol. 20 Johanna E. M. Schönrok: Innovation at Large. Managing Multi-Organization, Multi-Team Projects. 2010.

Band 21 Edda Behnken: Innovationsmanagement in Netzwerken. Analyse und Handlungskonzept zur kollektiven Innovationsgenerierung. 2010.

Vol. 22 Jan Wedemeier: Germany's Creative Sector and Its Impact on Employment Growth. A Theoretical and Empirical Approach to the Fuzzy Concept of Creativity: Richard Florida's Arguments Reconsidered. 2012.

www.peterlang.de